The Platinum Rule To Customer Service

"Treating Customers The Way They Want To Be Treated"

Authored By:

Sereva Ball, Brenda Carper, Michael DeSchalit,

David Erwin, Chad Froeschke, Pam Furlong, MJ Jensen,

Diane Kephart, Rick Moore, Pam Stewart, and Gaya Zeiter

DEDICATION AND ACKNOWLEDGMENTS

This book is dedicated to all of those that are in business to serve their customers according to the Platinum Rule of Customer Service. We would also like to recognize all the members of the Tucson Marketing Professionals, past, present and future who practice the highest standards of business and for their inspiration to publish this book in hopes of leading others to become experts in customer service. The contributing authors of this book wish to thank Chad Froeschke of WhiteSpace Design for designing the cover of this book and MJ Jensen of IdeaMagic visionary marketing & social media, our "Queen of Marketing", for her contribution in writing the forward to this book and her support of this collaborative project.

CONTENTS

FORWARD

As small business owners and entrepreneurs, our world is filled with "consultants" and people telling us what to do to grow our business. Rarely, do we find feet on the street, in the trenches, real advice from people who have actually experienced what it feels like to overcome the challenges of "successfully" running a small business.

Small business owners are just too darn busy to take time away from the demands of being the bookkeeper, the marketer, the social media manager, the employee babysitter, and the maintenance person to write a book. That is, until now. Michael has been our drill sergeant and our accountability person so we were motivated by his enthusiasm.

This book is filled with not just valuable advice, but with lessons of how we learned the hard way to overcome the day to day challenges of operating a small business.

My goal in contributing to this book was two-fold;

1) Help other small businesses avoid the pitfalls and mistakes that I made along the way.
2) Confirm that sometimes it's the simple things that matter the most in creating extraordinary customer service.

You will be reading about business owners that started from nothing and grew their business to a thriving entity and mostly because they were "Customer Laser Focused".

I have seen far too many business owners fail to see why their business failed. And it wasn't because of the economy. History has proven that businesses that take exceptional care of their customers and fill a need will survive during the darkest times in our country's economy.

I want to thank Michael DeSchalit for seeing the vision of collaboration and bringing the Tucson Marketing Professionals together to write this book. I hope it's the first of many. No other "networking" group has ever attempted this before so we are the Pioneers in transferring our knowledge to you in a way that we hope will resonate.

It has been an amazing ride being the "Leader" of Tucson Marketing Professionals and I don't see it ending any time soon. I'll be sharing my expertise as long as someone is willing to listen, learn and grow from my experiences.

Enthusiastically,

MJ Jensen, Chief Idea Officer, IdeaMagic visionary marketing & social media

And

The "Queen" of Tucson Marketing Professionals

1 INTRODUCTION

Customer service is something that just about every human being on this planet experiences in one way or another. Some of the customer service we experience is good, and in some case so good that it keeps us loyal to the one providing the service. It can even inspire us as business people to also provide that kind of great service to our clients and customers. In some cases, it can even inspire us, as people, to be kinder, more respectful and compassionate to everyone we encounter.

Then there is the other kind of customer service, or should I just say, lack of customer service. The inattentive server at a restaurant, the cranky medical assistant that leads us to the examination room, the rude clerk behind the counter at the Division of Motor Vehicle or the Post Office. We too, experience this kind of poor customer service from time to time in our lives, and as of late, more often than not are we treated to this lack of customer service. This is the kind of customer service that makes us choose to never frequent a restaurant again, dread going to the doctor or put off taking care of business at the DMV or the Post Office. This type of poor service, fortunately does not inspire us to treat others in the same way, but in some cases makes us mad; mad enough to commit to never treating our own people in the same bad way. That's right, this kind of poor customer service can inspire us to improve the way we treat our clients, customers and people in general.

So why is it that in a modern, technologically advanced, civil society such as ours do we find such a disparity? Why is there such a difference that spans the spectrum of total disregard for another human all the way to serving another as if they were a deity? I truly believe that the answer lies with a choice. That's right, a choice to be terrible and not care or a choice to be the best and to be a servant to others. I believe this to be true because even though we, as people, may come from different walks of life, different cultures, and different levels of education, being polite, caring and compassionate is something we all know how to do, but it's not always easy to follow through with. Yes, it does take extra effort, or at least effort to be those things, but it all starts with the choice to choose to put forth that effort.

In this book, you will meet several very successful business people who have devoted their careers, and in some cases their lives to being the best at customer service. This is something they have consciously made a decision to do in order to serve their clients and customers in such a way that the service level is beyond the golden rule. You know the golden rule; doing unto others the way you would have them do unto you, or as some interpret that to mean treat others the way you want to be treated. These are the business owners that practice "The Platinum Rule To Customer Service – *Treating Customers The Way They Want To Be Treated*". They go the extra distance and learn about their clients and customers, find out their likes and dislikes, build rapport and meaningful relationships, and then, once they know how their customers and clients want to be treated, they put all of their effort into treating them that way.

2 LET'S START WITH THE BASICS
AUTHOR: SEREVA BALL

In the month leading up to writing this chapter, I began reflecting on my own experiences with customer service and in the process, became more cognizant of how I was being treated as a customer – good, great, and bad. For weeks, I avoided writing – I was stumped, everyone knows how to give great customer service, right? How was I going to write a meaningful chapter about something people already know? But the more I reflected and observed, the more it became clear that it really isn't as obvious to everyone as I'd thought.

Let's start with the basics.

<u>Smile and be friendly.</u>

This seems pretty straightforward, but you'd be surprised (or maybe not?) at how often this one is overlooked.

A warm smile goes a long way and is quite noticeable when it's lacking. When someone smiles and is welcoming, I am immediately made to feel appreciated. I believe that they care about my experience, which helps me want to spend my hard earned money at their establishment. When someone is nice, it also makes it much easier to overlook small mistakes. I don't mean the kind where the new red car you ordered shows up blue, I mean the 'you got baked potatoes when you asked for mashed on a busy Friday night' kind. Conversely, the person who barely looks up from the computer (or phone) or even acknowledges my existence does not instill a lot of confidence that my business means anything to her. When mistakes are made, I assume it's because they don't care enough about me to do it right. I know the old adage is, 'It's not personal, it's business" but I don't think that could be more wrong. It's *always* personal.

Being friendly and welcoming is important, even in areas where you're not selling anything. An employee at our city's animal shelter recently received a lot of grief on Facebook because she was doing her work in the front reception area, answering texts and replying to emails via her phone. It was all business related and she doesn't have an office, but there was a line of people waiting to be helped, no one was at the front desk, and she didn't acknowledge a soul. People took her to task for being "a typical government worker." They even snapped photos of her, doing what looked to the average citizen like playing on her phone. It's so much easier to just treat people like you're glad they're there. When I taught school, if I was at the front office getting my mail, and the receptionist was briefly away from the desk, I always tried to at least recognize parents waiting at the front office. A simple, friendly "someone will be right with you" told them I saw them and was not ignoring them. That goes a long way. I'm much less apt to notice a wait at a restaurant table if my server stops by with a smile and "I'll be right back" rather than nothing at all. In my opinion, there is nothing worse than being ignored. It's insulting. It says, "you're not worthy of my time." To which my reply is, "you're not worthy of my money (or support)."

I know this book is about giving great customer service, but sometimes you need to recognize and ask yourself if the way you're behaving is worthy of great service. My first job was answering phones at a local manufacturing company during the summer. One day, a man called, insisting to speak to one of the workers in the plant. I explained that I would take a message and get it to him during his break. He started berating me, asking me if I knew who he was (I did, it was a small town.) I politely explained that this was the company policy. He screamed at me some more and when I still wouldn't budge, he demanded my name, including spelling. He then said, "Well Sereva, I think you just lost your job." Now, please remember I was only 16 years old, so give me a little latitude, but I smugly replied, "I don't think so. Would you like the spelling of my boss's name? It's Steve – last name spelled the same as mine. How about the company owner's name? His last name is spelled differently, but that's because he's my mom's dad." Silence, then 'click.'

I learned a valuable lesson at that man's expense. Never, ever treat someone like dirt because you assume they're a "nobody." You will never go wrong treating everyone like they're a CEO. I have a former boss, the executive director of a nonprofit I worked for, who used to answer the phone at the front desk whenever she was walking by. She confided that she learned a lot that way about the people she was dealing with.

Get to know your customers

I know in some fields that is more difficult than others. But I have to tell you, there is nothing cooler in the world than when my husband, KC, and I walk into our favorite Mexican restaurant on the south side and Jimmy, the owner, immediately grabs my husband's hand and says, "Great seeing you again, Mr. Ball," then nods his head and smiles at me, "Mrs. Ball." Admittedly, part of this is because Jimmy went to school with my father-in-law and my husband is the spitting image of his dad. But part of it is because we go there, a lot. It was where we went on our first date. Jimmy always asks KC about his mom and dad and often reminisces with him about his younger years. My husband is a detective and the last time we were there, he was on duty; which for him, means a shirt and tie with his gun and badge as accessories. It's a very popular restaurant, so even at lunchtime, we waited for a table because they have a strict 'no reservations' policy. (Even movie stars wait.) As we were paying, Jimmy said to KC, "I didn't realize you were working. Call me personally next time you're going to come in while you're on duty, I'll get you in right away." Then he handed my husband his card with his cell phone number. Now, I already think my husband is the s@%t, but that just confirmed it. Movie stars wait, we don't (at least when he's on duty). Boom. We live on the north side, there are plenty of Mexican restaurants close to us, but we've been driving 35 minutes, one-way, for over 20 years to go to this particular restaurant for a reason. The food is great but how special we are made to feel is priceless.

Care about meeting your customer's needs (and wants)

It's wonderful that I have my personal testimony to share with people about the products I sell. I often show my 'before' picture to people and am met with an incredulous, "That's you?" I do this to show the stuff really works; I'm walking proof. I first started using the line one summer while I was still teaching school. When I came back to work that August, several of my coworkers didn't recognize me. When they finally realized it was me, they wanted to know my secret. At that point, it was a no-brainer to become a distributor. As with many who are in direct sales, my first customers were friends and family. I had one friend tell me she was interested because she knew me and knew I was a 'no b.s. kind of girl.' So I have my reputation working for me, as well as my results, but not every person knows me or is looking to achieve results like I did. That's where 'knowing your customer' meets 'caring about her needs.' I was fortunate that, in the beginning, I already knew my customers. They felt comfortable telling me what they were looking for and since I was a product of my products, I could recommend things with confidence. I truly care about my customers and their results. Based on the number of referrals I get from existing clients, I think that is appreciated and apparent. If a customer isn't achieving the results she wants, I sit with her and try to pinpoint what she could do or try differently. I'm not a pushy, slick saleswoman. I'm much more of a "oh, by the way" kind of gal. An advantage to knowing your customers and caring about their needs is you can also recommend items they may not have asked about. For example, if I know Mrs. Jones' daughter is getting married, I can inquire about her stress levels (I have something to help with that), or simply suggest she and her bridesmaids have a wrap party to help them get ready for their dress shopping. Or I might learn her niece just had a baby and doesn't want to go back to work; I can offer the business opportunity so she can work from home.

One of the things that I most struggle with is assuming I already know someone's answer when I talk to them about the business or products. I'm working on that. Just because I *think* someone wouldn't be interested in what I have to offer, doesn't mean they aren't. I used to hate following up with leads. I'd psych myself out, convince myself they were going to be annoyed and think I was bothering them and be mean to me. I quickly realized after people were thanking *me* for calling *them*, that that line of thinking was all on me.

My little sister offered a great story from her own personal experience. She's a teacher and had a student she didn't know, but who was from her school, come to her classroom and ask her about buying raffle tickets for his group's fundraiser. She said she would, but could he come back the next day because she didn't have cash. The money is still in her desk, waiting for him to return. She wanted to buy the tickets, she had the means to buy the tickets, but she had no one to sell her the tickets. Don't be that guy. Follow up! Ask! I can't tell you how many times I would have had dessert, had the waitress not assumed I was done and brought the check. Bigger check equals bigger tip. I had a girlfriend tell me about a friend of ours who was also doing direct sales. She said he told her how great it worked, all the benefits, the cost, everything. But he never asked her to buy. She said she would have, but he just didn't present her with the opportunity.

Make them feel like a VIP

Years ago, when I was still in college, I used to drive 8 miles out of my way to go to a particular grocery store, bypassing other chains that were closer. I did this all because I had gone to this store one time when I was in the area and every store employee that I came in contact with took the time to stop, look at me, and ask with a smile if I needed any help. When I replied that I did, in fact, need help, I was taken to the item I needed. I wasn't given vague directions of, "it's on aisle 9." They asked if I had questions and I believed they genuinely cared if I did. They took my bags to the car. I thought I was being treated like a rock star! Me, a 23 years old student getting VIP treatment. And I never forgot it. I knew it was more expensive and I didn't even care – I loved how they made me feel. From that day forward, I shopped there faithfully for seven years. When my husband and I moved to our new house with our kids, I was so happy that it was closer. It was still not the closest supermarket, but it was less of a drive. One Sunday evening, after 90 minutes of grocery shopping, I was checking out and the cashier wouldn't take my check because it was over $300 (those were the days before debit cards). Embarrassed, I explained that I wrote checks there all the time, that I'd never bounced a check in my life, and that my account had plenty of money. When the manager came over, I went through my spiel again, this time adding that my total was frequently over $300 (we have three kids) and there'd never been a problem before. She told me she could see my check history and totals going back several years (and even gave me a print out – big mistake) and that everything I was telling them was true but the manager (who was new) still refused to accept my check. I learned from the print out that over those few years, I had written more than $13,000 worth of checks to that store. I never went back after that night. I decided if I was going to be humiliated and made to feel ordinary, I could do it for a lot cheaper and closer to my house.

I can't emphasize this enough, treat everyone like a rock star - always.

Lastly, make sure all your employees are doing the same

When I was teaching, I had a student whose father was an executive for one of the casinos in town. When the student graduated, they gave me an incredible gift of a two-night stay at his casino's hotel and a dining credit. KC and I decided to go on my birthday weekend. The hotel was amazing; it was brand new and everything was first-rate: the lobby, the rooms, the pool - even the elevator areas - all gorgeous. On my actual birthday, we decided to rent one of the cabanas by the pool. This was something we'd never done before but I'd always wanted to do. I remembered how I would sit longingly watching the people being waited on in their beautiful, shaded areas with couches, radios, TVs, and misters, thinking, "THAT is the life." It always just seemed too excessive for my salary, but it was my birthday and our hotel room was paid for so we decided to splurge. Our kids drove to the hotel to spend the day by the pool with us. The hospitality manager brought out a cake and helped sing happy birthday to me. It should have been the perfect day. Unfortunately, the waiter at our cabana was awful. I mean horrible. Not just by giving terrible service, but he was rude, arrogant, and spiteful. The worst time I've ever had in my life. Whenever I think about returning there, all I can think of is my experience with him and how he took a special day that was supposed to be wonderful and ruined it, purposefully. I doubt I will ever go back, regardless of how beautiful the hotel or how nice (or apologetic) the hospitality manager. All because of how someone on their frontline regarded me.

People always say, "Treat people the way you want to be treated," but I don't think that goes far enough. I say, treat people the way you would if your best friend from high school became a famous actress and was thinking about becoming your customer. You'd be warm, friendly, and enthusiastic. You'd let her know how much you appreciated her for thinking of you and your company. You'd reply promptly to any questions she had. You'd take the time to listen to what she needed, then provide her with your best quality product or service to meet those needs. You'd double-check everything. If there were obstacles, you'd find a way around them. You'd go out of your way to make sure she was satisfied, then you'd follow up just to be certain she was happy. You'd also make dang sure any employee of yours knew to also treat her with kid gloves.

If you aren't already doing this for every client you have, my only question is – why not?

Sereva Ball is the married mother of three children. She and her family used to foster dogs until her husband realized she was really bad at it (dogs were coming in, but none were leaving!), so they also share their home with six dogs. Prior to working in education, Sereva was part of the business world, employed in both the public and private sector. When her children arrived, she went back to school for her Master's degree and became a special education teacher; a career she had for 14 years before embarking on a new chapter. Sereva is now a distributor for It Works! Global; specializing in helping people look good and feel great with body wraps and health supplements. Check out her It Works line at SerevaBall.com.

Having a strong It Works team has allowed her to follow her passion of writing. As a professional writer, she not only is a ghost blogger for other companies and people, but she also maintains two personal blogs. PepperandPals.blogspot.com is about her life as a mom, dog foster failure, and wife of a police officer, and in AnotherMSMoment.com, she chronicles her experiences with Multiple Sclerosis, a disease she was officially diagnosed with in 2009.

You can reach her at SerevaBall@gmail.com

3 THE CUSTOMER SERVICE SNOB
AUTHOR: BRENDA CARPER

Is there such a thing as a Customer Service snob? There is, and I am proud to say that I am one of them.

I consider customer service and how one treats their employees, peers, vendors and customers the most important part of business success or failure. People can make you or break you. It is one's ability to be proactive and how they are reactive that will make the difference between service success or failure. Because I am a customer service snob, I tend to consider how I am being treated and what my customer experience is everywhere I go. We tend to think of customer service only in the aspect of the customer who walks through the door. When in fact everyone around you is a customer. One has to carefully consider their actions and reactions on every level.

Social Media has really changed how one should think about customer service. Service issues and how they are handled can make or break a company. In the old days when social media did not exist, if a customer had a service issue they may have just told a few people. Today if there is a service situation no matter who may be right or wrong, the customer is posting their experience on Facebook, Twitter and Instagram at minimum. They are probably posting while in your presence and maybe even snapping a photo of you. Smile!! Your picture along with some choice words for your company are being blasted to millions across the world. Think about the damage this can cause a company. It could potentially shut you down. No one wants to do business with an organization that does not treat their customers well. You will probably even be tagged to see what your response will be. How will you handle it? Could this have been avoided? Were there steps that could have been taken to empower your employees to make good customer service decisions? People will be watching to see how you react. It is an opportunity for you to take a bad situation and turn it to gold with how you respond.

Customer service is driven from the top down. Employee satisfaction is directly tied in with customer satisfaction. Employees and managers that are engaged and made to feel they make a difference in their organizations are more apt to care about losing a customer or client. Employees and managers must also be trained and be empowered to be able to make critical decisions at a moment's notice. They should feel free to make decisions in regards to service without worrying about what the ramifications might be. If needed, set parameters. No one plans to give the farm away. It just makes sense for employees to make decisions at the moment the service error is occurring. They need to be trained to think outside the box. Service can be recovered and given in a variety of ways and it does not always have to cost the company money. A leader must set the standards. Would it not be great for someone to say "this is how I can fix this", instead of "I have to go my boss and they have to go to their boss until a solution can be found. The worst response is "I can't help you" or "there is nothing I can do". The world is not all black and white. It is a million shades of gray and there is always a solution. It is what you say and how you say it that can make all the difference in the world, even if the answer is not what the customer wants to hear. Training and role playing can help employees learn various techniques to handle different situations. Service should be at the forefront of what your company represents. Customer service is an art. It takes time and patience to develop the talent. Customer Service is always a work in progress. There are several standards that I live by to ensure customer service success. As a small business owner I follow these rules to ensure my clients and customers are happy.

Here are some important rules to follow.

Acknowledgement- How long does a person have to wait to be acknowledged? Customer service should start at the door. As a customer service snob who likes to be noticed, this is one of my top five pet peeves. I see this on a consistent basis everywhere I go and in almost every industry. I will walk into an office, flash a smile that says yes I am ready for your help and then nothing! So annoying! Sometimes people will look at you and seem annoyed that you had the nerve to even come through the door. Nothing feels more frustrating when your plan is to spend money in that organization. Rule number #1: Acknowledgement. Please remember to stand up, smile, shake the customer's hand and thank them for being there. I recently had to visit an auto store to buy $800 worth of parts for my car. I walked in; no one greeted me or said hi. I stood there for at least 20 minutes and nothing. There had to have been at least 6 employees working in the store. Granted they were busy and I understood that but the fact they walked by me every 5 seconds and never said a word was so frustrating. I walked away a very unhappy customer. All they had to do was acknowledge me smile and say they would be with me shortly. That would have made all the difference in the world. No acknowledgement made me feel like they were trying to hide from me in hopes that I might leave because they were so busy. In today's world, emails can also serve as a form of acknowledgement. It is really difficult to respond to each email you receive. The person on the other end is waiting for a quick response. We have started to implement email rules in my company; remember co-workers are also the beneficiary of bad service. We were finding that emails were not being responded to or that something urgent was not being addressed. In addition to the internal emails, we have external emails come in for our services that we need to respond to. Now when we send emails to each other we code the subject line so we know if we need to respond and how quickly. FYI means just sending for your information; you do not need to respond. Urgent means this is urgent and response needed as soon as possible. Response needed means this email is not urgent but I do need you to eventually respond.   If I can't commit to a full response to customers and clients right away, I will respond and ask if it is ok if I get back to them in 24 hours or I will call them this afternoon. This way it is acknowledgement that you have received the email and you plan to respond soon. I also think we have phones for a reason. We sometimes use email as a crutch to avoid having an actual conversations with people. I will pick up the phone if I think the email thread is going to go on too long or if I think the person on the other end may be unsure of the tone of the emails. A phone call can add a more personal touch.

Perception- At the early start of my career a wise manager told me perception is reality. Sometimes it does not matter what the truths are because the customer's perception is what matters. This always stuck with me. So now in every situation I remember that and I make an effort to put myself in their shoes and experience the situation from their side. No matter what the truth of the situation is, how they are perceiving it is the reality for them.

Listen- Are you listening to me? In sales and service I often find that people have their own agendas and ideas on how things should happen. Stop selling! Listen. If you really want to sell something take time to get to know the customer. Find out what they need, and build a relationship.   How can you know what your customers and client's needs are unless you are listening? Take time to get to know the people you are working with. How can you provide good service if you have no idea what the end goal is of the person you are talking to. Treat people how they want to be treated not how you think they should be treated. Don't pretend to listen while thinking only of how you will close the deal. Really listen! I recently went to a furniture store to buy a new headboard. I knew in my mind the look and the color I wanted for my room. I told the sales person my room was grey and white tones and my furniture and flooring were of darker wood. He showed me some headboards based on what I asked for. We looked at all the styles of the type of headboard I was looking for and I let him know right away the ones I was not interested in at all. Finally we came across a beautiful dark grey headboard that I knew would look fabulous in my room. I was so excited!! I said "I will take it" and he was off to put the order in. A few minutes later he came over and apologized that the particular headboard was closed out in the King size and no other store had it available. I was really sad. As I was about to leave, he said we do have it in the Queen size. Did he not hear me say I had a king bed? I reminded him quickly and he said "I am sure it will not look that bad". I said "I am not interested". I then told him I had to pick up my child at a party shortly and that I was sorry it did not work out. At that point, he tried to get me to consider the other headboards we looked at. I said, "No if you recall I did not like any of those and they would not look good in my room". He then said "We can get the bed you like in beige. I am sure that will look great in your room". I politely told him I really wanted grey and that I was not sure I would like beige. He proceeded to badger and insist that I consider it. At this point, I was becoming very frustrated. I finally had to become an angry customer and tell him I was not interested in anything else as I walked out the door. I left feeling very frustrated because I was not heard. I felt this person did not value me. They just valued the sale. It will be a while before I shop there again. If he had listened and said, "I am sorry we could not help, but I know what you are looking for. I will search other stores and keep my eye out for what you are looking for", my customer experience would have been so much different. I would have walked away impressed and I probably would have gone back the next week to see if anything new came in. Just Listen!

Responsibility- It is not my fault, it is everyone else's!! Heard that before? Why is it so hard for someone to take responsibility for their actions and the actions of others? Customers do not care if your vendor dropped the ball or if someone in operations forgot to put in an order. The end result, no matter how it happened, is that the customer is not happy with the outcome. In the end you are responsible because you are the one in front of the customer or client. I find it sad when people use their co-workers, their company or vendors as a scapegoat and excuse. Even if it was an error from one of these parties, the customer does not need to know. They do not care. They just want their issue resolved. Everyone is human and everyone makes mistakes. I think most people will understand this and are impressed when you just admit the error and provide an immediate solution. For instance, I recently received an email from my daughter's principal in regards to the 8th grade graduation. The principal had made the decision to separate the graduation into two groups; one in the morning and one in the afternoon. I am sure there were several factors in regards to making this decision. The students were very upset, and a protest was in the works. A few days later we received an email from the principal. The principal admitted to making a mistake; he did not consider the students would be upset with his actions and it did not occur to him to ask. He did not realize how important it was for the students to graduate together and he apologized to everyone: students, parents and staff. He said this year 8th grade graduation would go unchanged. Next year he would put together a committee of students, staff and parents for graduation to make decisions on needed changes. He could have easily ignored the situation and went on with his plan. He chose to take the high road, admit he was wrong and came up with a resolution that would include everyone. I almost teared up when I read the email. I had found another customer service snob! Acknowledge a mistake has been made and that you were a part of that mistake. Come up with a solution and include the other party in that solution. You may not be able to meet eye to eye but making the attempt to include them will make the person on the other side feel like you value them and that they have some control in the situation.

Pride-   I recall early in my career in customer service I felt very protective of the companies I worked for. Now that I have my own company, I have come to realize that while I still feel protective the overall goal is to attract and retain customers and clients and that I need to do everything in my power to make the customer happy, especially in today's age of social media. They just can't wait to let the world know how horrible you are to do business with and people listen! Always consider if you have done everything you can to make the customer happy, and if not, what the ramifications may be. Of course it is hard to do that in the heat of the moment. It takes discipline and practice, but it is a must if you want to be successful. I think it is ingrained in people to be on the defensive.   I often find in service glitches that people immediately feel the need to prove they are right or have not made a mistake. It becomes a battle as to who can prove their point. In the end no one wins. Everyone walks away frustrated. Humans have a tendency to take situations to heart. It is hard to take a step back, breathe and say to yourself "is this worth it". Granted many times the customer can be wrong. Consider that arguing and trying to prove a point is not a good use of your time or theirs. Consider the big picture. Sometimes people just want to be heard and when they are, it will diffuse the situation. Acknowledge the issue, offer solutions and move on. Do this with pride in yourself and your company.

Expectations and Standards- Set the standards and expectations for your clients. Don't oversell and over promise on items you may not be able to deliver. Explain processes to people so they have a complete understanding how things work. Set the expectation with clients and customers so they are not caught off guard and they understand their role in the process. Ask if they have questions. It is important to admit when you are not sure of something and then let them know you will get back to them. I often find that if I am told up front what to expect, I am not upset if there is a delay. After all, I was warned. Many service glitches can be diffused if expectations are set and a customer has a good understanding of the rules and expectations.

Be proactive- Anticipate potential issues. This can sometimes be tedious and boring work but it can save you from difficult customer issues later on. We do corporate housing and one of the big potential issues for our clients is a key missing from a lockbox. Can you imagine traveling across the country, having to find a location in the middle of the night and then finally finding your apartment but the key to get into the apartment is not there? Could you imagine how angry you might be? This happened early in my career. I happened to be on pager duty that night and I got the emergency call that the client could not get into the accommodations. We could not reach anyone at the property to let them in. I decided to see if we had another unit available at the same property that we could put him into for the night. Sure enough we did. I gave the guest the lockbox code to that accommodation. I thought everything was great and then got another emergency call. Someone was already in that unit! The client in that unit decided to check in a few days early without notifying us. The original guest was beyond frustrated at this point and I was too. I felt that my team had let me and our customer down. How could someone miss a key in a lockbox? What process and procedure were in place? I apologized profusely for our error. The customer was very angry and vented his anger to me. I let him. I stayed quiet and simply listened. I did not interrupt, offer excuses, nor blame my team. This customer just needed someone to listen to his ordeal and how angry he was. After he was done yelling, I told him at this point it would probably be best if we checked him into a hotel. I told him I would meet him at a hotel close to where he was at. I speed across town to get there as quickly as possible. I was worried on the way that he would yell and scream and cause a scene when I got there. He did the opposite. He gave me a huge hug and apologized for cursing and yelling at me earlier. He said he was sorry he took his frustration out on me. He calmed down after he was able to vent with me on the phone and appreciated I just listened and made no excuses. We became good friends after that. This is why it is important to have checks and balances and policies and procedures in place to ensure that glitches such as these are avoided. It is impossible to anticipate everything but steps can be taken for quality control. When I started my company, making sure keys were in the lockbox was a top priority. We set up processes to double and even triple check various steps in the check-in process with written and photo documentation that helps to avoid these types of issues. We anticipate issues that may arise and find solutions to prevent them from happening.

Customer Service Snob- yes indeed! The excellent customer service you give your clients and customers by being responsive and responsible will keep them returning to your business.

Brenda Carper is a Tucson Native. She graduated from Canyon Del Oro High School and attended Pima Community College and The University of Arizona. She is currently a member of Tucson Marketing Professionals, Arizona Business Travel Association and The Corporate Housing Providers Association. Brenda owns, and is designated broker for Arizona Housing Solutions, LLC. Arizona Housing Solutions specializes in furnished property management, real estate sales and furnished temporary housing in Tucson and Phoenix. You can reach her at 520-449-3706, brenda@azhousingsolution.com or www.azhousingsolution.com.

4 SUPER STAR OR SUPER SERVANT?
AUTHOR: MICHAEL DESCHALIT

It just seems as though it's getting worse. Everywhere we go, whether it's at a restaurant, a grocery store or the airport, customer service is at an all-time low. Now those are not my words, but in fact the words of my teenage daughter. Yeah, pretty scary huh when a teenager is noticing it at those places, at her age? Well, I have to admit, she's not your ordinary run of the mill teenager... she's my daughter. This is a girl who has grown up with me as her dad never having what we would call a "Real Job", meaning that I am self-employed. Because of that experience, she has been able to observe to what ends I am willing to go to find, gain and retain my clients. She recognizes that I am able to do this by providing excellent customer service to all of my clients and even prospective clients.

My business is multi-faceted; I am a Comedy Hypnotist, a Magician, a Motivational Speaker and a Clinical Hypnotherapist. In all of those businesses, I serve others. Whether it be by making them laugh at one of my shows, inspire them with a presentation, or help them change their life in my hypnotherapy office; I serve others. I have been self-employed for about twenty years in these professions and have learned, sometimes via the college of hard knocks, about how to treat my clients, or should I say how my clients want to be treated. You see the latter is far better than the former. To provide the best customer service, it is imperative that you find out HOW your customers WANT to be treated as opposed to treated them how you THINK they want to be treated. This is why I like the title of this book so much because treating your customers the way they want to be treated is The Platinum Rule. The Golden Rule says to do unto others the way you would have them do unto you. I interpret that to mean treat others the way you want to be treated. The flaw in that is that not everyone wants to be treated the way you want to be treated. Most people would much rather that you get to know them as a person and then treat them with respect, which is then the WAY they want to be treated. All of that being considered let's take a look at how that process works.

In the late seventies and early eighties, a new type of selling strategy was implemented. It was called "Needs Based Selling". In this sales method, a salesperson did not just try to cram a product or service down the throats of any person who was willing to listen to a sales pitch. In fact, it worked just the opposite. Sales people would prospect to markets or groups of people who they thought might need or want a particular product or service. Once they found a prospect that was willing to listen to the "pitch", they would first pre-qualify that person to see if they in fact were really interested in the product or service and were ready to "buy". This saved the sales people and the prospects a lot of frustration and time listening to pointless sales pitches and actually helped sales people close more deals with more satisfied customers. So how did they do this? It's actually a very simple process and the first step to providing Platinum Level Customer Service… They get to know the customer, they build rapport, they listen, and they learn how the customer WANTS to be treated.

So let's take a closer look at this process… First, getting to know the customer, or as it is sometimes referred to, building rapport. This is a process that I am very familiar with as a hypnotist. You see, it is impossible to hypnotize anyone without their consent, or without their trust in you, the hypnotist. In essence, this is rapport. The only real way of gaining rapport is to spend time, quality time, with someone and by getting to know their wants and needs. This means that there are no assumptions made, only fact gathering. This is accomplished by talking with your prospect (soon to be customer or client) and asking them questions about themselves. What they like, what they don't like, what they need, want they are looking for in this relationship (with you). The last one is the important one. What do they want out of this relationship with you (and your business, product or service)? When you can get this information, you will begin to build rapport and you will begin to earn their trust. When you are asking them questions, however, it must not be an interrogation. You must be genuinely interested in what they have to say… YOU MUST BE A GOOD LISTENER!!! This is not something that most people are good at, but this skill can be learned and mastered. You must always remember that God gave us two ears and one mouth so that we can listen twice as much as we speak. I can't honestly remember who first said that, but it is so true. Listening is a learned skill. Now to become a master of that skill, as I mentioned, you must be genuinely interested in the person you are listening to. Not just because they are a prospective client and a potential source of future revenue, but because YOU honestly and earnestly are so passionate about your business, product or service that you want to share it with those who you feel it will enhance their life in some way or another. That's right, it starts with you. Are you so passionate about your business that you want to share it with others to enhance their lives and make this world a better place? I certainly hope so. I believe that you do, otherwise you probably wouldn't be reading this book looking for ways in which to improve yourself. So, knowing that you are passionate about what you do, you must remember to listen with empathetic ears. This will allow you to only hear what the prospect or your client is really feeling, what their TRUE wants and needs are.

Once you have established rapport, you will then begin down the road of building trust with your prospects, customers and clients. This process is a never ending process and must be maintained and never violated lest the relationship will be forever damaged. It's ironic that building trust is one of the most difficult things to do with another person, but tearing down that trust can only take a second, a word or a single action. A lot of business people will tell you that people do business with people they know, like and TRUST. Well, you've gotten to know them, they must like you because they are still with you, but do they trust you? At what point do they trust you enough to subscribe to your business, product or service? I'm sure that as each and every person in the world is different, there are as many different levels of trust and times when a person decides to trust another. So how can we best insure that they will be open to the possibility of trusting you enough to subscribe to your business, product or service? The best method I know of is by communicating with them. Yeah, I know you have already been doing that. After all you can't get to know someone if you don't communicate with them. But remember, up to this point, your role has been more of a listener and the only talking you have been doing is the questions you have been asking them to learn about them. So now is your chance to share what you have to share.

So when I say, you must communicate with them, I really mean this... You must be open, honest, upfront, clear and direct with them... on all levels of the relationship. Let me explain the "all levels of the relationship" part first and then I'll come back to the other facets. All levels of the relationship mean that over time, if you do a great job at being a super servant to this customer or client, they will have different levels of a relationship with you. They will see you as the provider of the business, product or service you are giving them, but they will also see you as a friend or confidant and someone they will introduce to their sphere of influence, such as family and friends (and their business colleagues) and will ultimately refer your business, product or service to others. Your honesty and integrity must always be present in every level of this relationship. So how do you accomplish this? Again, it's not difficult; you just must always be upfront with them. When you are explaining your business, product or service, you explain how it works and then make sure they understand all that they need to work with you and to have a healthy business relationship with you. Answer any questions or concerns they might have before you begin working with them and at any time during the process of your working relationship with them. Especially address the concerns! Upfront! Head-On! Let's face it, we all make mistakes and we all have things that go wrong with our business, products or services from time to time. Sometimes those are within our control but most of the time they are not. Honestly is the best policy in all situations. If something goes bad, address it immediately, be honest and upfront and then do everything in your power to rectify the situation... ALWAYS DO THE RIGHT THING... A-L-W-A-Y-S!!! There can be no exceptions to this rule, ever. Now there are times when you have a bad situation arise and then you do the right thing to fix it, you might still lose the customer or client. But, you won't compromise your own values. It will be painful, it will hurt (emotionally and sometimes financially) but you will come away with knowledge and peace knowing you did the right thing. Open, good, honest communication is what every customer and client deserves. When communicating to your customers or clients you too must remember to always be clear and concise; communicate in terms with them that they understand. Using jargon and confusing terms that they don't understand, whether intentional or not, more often than not lead to disastrous results later on down the road. Remember, it only takes a second to destroy trust.

Once you have gotten to this point where you have spent the necessary time to get to know your customer or client, built trust with them and communicate your business, product or service to them, you must now maintain this relationship. This is where a lot of businesses begin to fail. They figure that they've got you, so they don't have to work at the relationship any more. Such a big mistake!!!

DON'T make this mistake!!! This part of customer service is actually the hardest part, or at least takes the most intentional work. Note, I said intentional. That's right; you have to work at it. You have to INTENTIONALLY set aside time and energy to maintain the relationship. You must continue to practice all of the steps we talked about earlier in this chapter as far as continuing to build rapport and trust. As for communication, you must constantly make sure, as the business relationship grows, that there aren't any new questions or ambiguities that arise that if left unanswered could lead to the rapport or trust being damaged. In many types of businesses, the majority of communication happens on the front end of the relationship, in as much as, the major issues are handled as the relationship is being established. After that as things are rolling along, it's very easy for us to fall victim to directing our attention to new customers or clients and then, unintentionally, neglecting our established customers or clients. Out of sight, out of mind, right? Maybe we aren't seeing our existing customers or clients with the same frequency as a new customer, client or prospect; or maybe we allow one of our staff to handle the existing customer base and they drop the ball; or worse, we just get too busy to handle it all. So to avoid this pitfall, you must set up a system in which you set aside time daily, weekly or monthly (even quarterly or yearly if that is enough) when you can reach out to your customer or client base to let them know you haven't forgot about them. This also works great with customers or clients that you have completed working with as they can be the best source of referrals for your business. The contact you make with your customers or clients in this part of the process doesn't have to be elaborate or even very time consuming. This point of contact can be as simple as an email, a newsletter (that they give permission to receive – otherwise, this is known as stalking), a greeting card or a quick phone call to say "Hi, I just wanted to check in to see how you are doing". I call my clients and say "I'm just calling to give you a check-up from the neck up". It gets a laugh and lets them know that I do care. So stay in touch and let your customers and clients know that you do still care and you weren't just after their business or their money.

After doing all of these steps with every customer or client every time, you will find that this process becomes natural and you can do it effortlessly and easily. It does take work, but then again everything that's worth doing takes work. But with your passion for what you do, your business, product or service, this becomes a labor of love. You see, it really is about attitude and choice. You begin by making a choice to be a Super Servant not a Super Star. I was fortunate to learn this early on in my professional life. I have been blessed with the opportunity to have received a litany of awards in all of my endeavors, Hypnosis, Magic, Speaking and my work in Hypnotherapy. I have walls that are covered with certificates, accolades and plaques, but the only reason I display them is as a reminder that I have made the choice to be a Super Servant, not a Super Star. Because you see, I only have all of those trophies because of the customers and clients that I have had the pleasure of working with on this journey. So I will leave you with these final thoughts... Make the choice to offer Platinum Level Customer Service. Meet and greet your customers and clients with a smile on your face and an open heart, get to know them, earn their trust, work hard to maintain that trust, communicate openly, honestly and truthfully at all times, Always do the right thing even when it's hard, never cease to work diligently at staying in touch with your customers and clients and most of all always strive to be a Super Servant.

Here are a few extra tips that I have found that help convey to your customers, clients and prospects that you really care about them...

1) Always answer your phone (when you are able). If they are calling you, it MUST BE important. Don't subscribe to the ridiculous philosophy that if you let it go to voicemail, they will think you are so busy because you are so successful that

they will definitely want to work with you. That's ridiculous... when you don't answer; they will simply go somewhere else.

2) Always be polite. Okay I know... the customer is NOT ALWAYS right. This may be true, but this is also true... They are profit, you are overhead. Treat them with respect and dignity at all times, even when they are wrong. Also, don't forget to say please and thank you. Those words cost you nothing but will gain you everything.

3) Always return phone calls, emails, messages or texts. Let me say that again. ALWAYS RETURN PHONE CALLS, EMAILS, MESSAGES AND TEXTS!!! If you don't return these calls, emails, messages or texts in a timely manner, you may as well just tell them that you don't care. This is perhaps the rudest thing you can do and the boldest way to show someone how little you care about them and how unimportant and insignificant they are to you by not taking a minute or two of your time to return a call, email, message or text. Yes, this is my pet peeve!!!

Michael is a graduate of the University of Arizona with a degree in sociology, emphasizing group dynamics. In addition to being a Nationally Certified Motivational Speaker, Trainer and Facilitator, Michael is a Certified Clinical Hypnotherapist, Comedy Stage Hypnotist, Professional Magician and Published Author. Over the past 20 years he has performed for and presented to over 750,000 students, teachers and business professionals in twenty-three states in four countries and on two continents. He has designed, written and implemented dozens of seminars, he is a multi-award winning magician and he was the recipient of the "Hypnotism Achievement Award" in 2013. He is the owner of Magically Speaking, LLC and operates Motivating Minds Hypnosis Center in Tucson, Arizona.

Michael C. DeSchalit

www.motivatingmindshypnosis.com

www.thehypnozone.com

www.magicallyspeaking.net

(520)270-0183

motivatingmindshypnosis@gmail.com

5 LEADERSHIP, CULTURE & CUSTOMER SERVICE EXCELLENCE
AUTHOR: DAVID ERWIN

When people hear the phrase customer service, an image or an idea of what is right and wrong springs to our minds. When it comes to building a business that relies on customer service to retain clients (What organization doesn't rely on this?), we must realize that how we serve our customers (external and internal) is a direct reflection of our organizational culture and its leadership.

Most people think that leadership is about authority. In fact, according to John C. Maxwell, leadership is nothing more and nothing less than influence.

Influence is defined as: the action or process of producing effects on the actions, behavior, opinions, etc., of another or others.

Customer service is a leadership skill that must be trained, practiced, evaluated, and coached to excellence so that employees represent the company in the brightest possible light.

The core of the word service is serve, which in its purest form means to serve others. In Robert Greenleaf's book, Servant Leadership, the goal of customer service is "to make them better" than when the encounter began.

If you are a customer service representative, and let's be honest every single team member is, then you are the face of that company or organization. As such, you have an opportunity to demonstrate the "servant-hood" attitude in every customer interaction.

What we are talking about is leaving an impression on our customers about the importance and value we place on them, a snapshot of our organizational culture if you will.

As an impressionable kid I heard the old adage, "the customer is always right."

This philosophy was coined by Marshall Field (the founder of Marshall Field's department store) in the earliest part of the twentieth-century and quickly swept through the country as the standard for customer service excellence. Of course, Field didn't intend this to be taken literally. What he was attempting to do was to make the customer feel special by impressing upon the staff the disposition to behave as if the customer was right, even when they weren't.

In my early days as a consumer, I took this impression to heart and used it as my golden ticket: "I have the right to have things my way, and you are going to give it to me!" Many times, I found myself being a bully with a customer service representative in order to obtain what I was promised, "the customer is always right!"

What kind of impression do you imagine I left?

Many times, the customer is absolutely right, other times they are not: either way our goal as a leader of customer service is to find that win-win solution; one which will empower the customer as well as the customer-service representative.

I'll never forget my first official train-the-trainer workshop I attended well over twenty years ago. I was so excited to finally have found my purpose and to have taken the first steps; I was absorbing everything like a sponge. Our facilitators were Sam Sikes, Mary Butler, and Glen Olson. One of the first things that I really connected with is the advice that Sam shared with our group:

- Always understand why you are doing what you are doing
- Always model the behavior you expect from your group

So, what does this have to do with customer service?

As leaders, our role is to set the standards for creating and maintaining our culture. To build a culture that creates other leaders who are driven by Customer Service Excellence, we must do what it takes to ensure our culture is built upon a solid foundation. To do this we need to outline the "why" behind our actions, then through modeling, training, coaching and mentoring help our team members embrace this as well.

Secondly, as leaders, we must walk-the-talk at all times. We are responsible for the message we send. If we do not, we are setting everything and everyone up for failure.

Below you will find a blueprint for creating a culture of leaders working towards customer service excellence that will set your organization apart from the crowd.

First decide to create then commit to a culture of Customer Service Excellence:

At Leader Within Us, we define culture as "the way things are around here - culture is both written and unwritten rules, attitudes, customs, rituals, and values shared by the members of an organization that are impressed upon and accepted by new members."

When we are talking about organizational culture, this is something that must be created with forethought, planning, and deliberate actions.

The leadership team must create and embody their vision for customer service excellence. Our customers are savvy, know what they want, and expect us to live up to our promises.

Dr. Leonard L. Barry, who is a former Professor of Marketing at Texas A & M University cites, "Customer expectations of service organizations are loud and clear: look good, be responsive, be reassuring through courtesy and competence, be empathetic, but most of all, be reliable. Do what you said you would do. Keep the service promise."

The customer service experience is very personal. When I take the time to put myself in the shoes of my customer and feel what they are experiencing, it allows for a greater connection and desire to resolve their issue.

Leaders of an organization must decide that customer service will be the top value, not just a priority.

Here's the difference between the two: Priorities change; values never will.

As a speaker, coach and facilitator I spend roughly 80% of my days on the road working with clients. As you can imagine, taking care of myself while traveling can be a bit of a challenge, at best. Last night I decided that I'd get up this morning at 4:30, get in a good workout, eat breakfast, and then head to the course-room by 7:00. What actually happened is, I repeatedly hit "snooze" on my phone and didn't crawl out of bed until 6:30.

So, was getting up at 4:30 a value or priority?

If it had been a value, I 'd have been in the gym by 4:45.

Speaking of values, one thing I cannot stress enough, is that our customers are not just people outside of our doors, on the other end of the phone or email; our Customer Service Excellence must begin internally. This way it permeates the culture at all levels. When we (organizationally) live the values we tell our customers we are about there are no gaps in performance, beliefs or actions.

To ensure this level of permeation every single member of the organization must be held accountable for his or her actions. This can be uncomfortable. Holding anyone accountable can be daunting and intimidating. Magnify that by 1000 when it comes to senior team members, but it must be done for this to work – we are all in this together.

What happens to a culture when we have flexible expectations? When we have different expectations (rules) for different people within the organization, people see this; people talk; productivity drops; morale plummets.

Can you recall a time you've experienced this?

Hire the right people:

One of my favorite books is Good to Great, by Jim Collins. In his book he states, "Greatness is not a function of circumstance. Greatness, it turns out, is largely a matter of conscious choice and discipline."

As leaders, it's our job to get the right people on board and in the right seats. Like creating a foundation for the culture, it should be done with forethought and deliberate action. You will have to decide as a leadership team the characteristics you want in your people.

Here are a few winning characteristics I have encountered over the years:

- People who genuinely like people
- People who are willing to learn, grow and stretch beyond what they know
- People who are dedicated to being in service
- People who are willing to give and receive feedback
- People who are willing to be held and are willing to hold others accountable
- People who have a proven track record in customer service
- People who are self-aware, humble and willing to learn from their mistakes
- People who are willing to develop themselves as leaders
- People who are committed to doing the right thing

When we prioritize on-boarding the right people, we set our customers and our organization up for success; this must be a deliberate process that is planned and thoroughly executed.

Orientation and Training:

Charles F. Kettering writes, "High achievement always takes place in the framework of high expectation."

Once we get the right people on the bus and in the right seats, then the real work begins. Orientation and training is something that most organizations just "tick-the-box" and call it done. When you take time to deliberately facilitate the new hire orientation and train them in customer service, you create the opportunity to:

- Identify customer service expectations
- Model what great customer service looks like
- Get the purpose of their role in the organization across straight away
- You'll create buy-in and have people competing to go the extra mile
- They will know exactly what it is they are being paid to do

The modern-day founder of Ritz-Carlton makes certain that he is at every new hotel opening and is facilitating the orientation personally. He doesn't speak of the day-to-day aspects of their jobs (e.g., restaurant and bar menus, housekeeping roles and responsibilities, etc.), he takes time to clearly outline the purpose of each and every person employed with Ritz-Carlton.

He tells them up front, "I am the president of this hotel. I am an important person around here."

He continues, " You are an important person too – you control the impression the guests have of the hotel more than I ever could."

He spells out their purpose as: "The genuine care and comfort of our guests is our highest mission."

What kind of impression has he made upon his staff?

The creed of all employees of Ritz-Carlton is, "If I see it, I own it." Every employee, should they have a concern brought to his or her attention by a guest, must see it through until the guest is fully satisfied. The same thing applies to issues with the property (e.g., maintenance, cleanliness, etc.): he or she must see it through until the issue has been resolved properly.

There is no room for, "It's not my job!" in an organization which prioritizes leading customer service excellence.

Coaching and Mentoring:

Once you have spent the necessary time to orient and train your people, it's time to let them spread their wings. This time could be called an internship (or learning time) of sorts. It's a time of:

- Learning by doing
- Coming into contact with the customers and learning what they really need
- Finding out what works and doesn't work
- Making mistakes
- Learning what you don't know

This time can be incredibly stressful and discouraging, especially in the beginning. It can also be exciting and empowering. If discouragement is allowed to take root, you will experience avoidable washout from your training class. As leaders, this is where we must jump in with questions, encouragement, coaching and mentoring.

What's the difference between mentoring and coaching? It's really pretty simple: Coaching focuses on performance issues and Mentoring focuses on the individual. Coaching is short term and task focused. Mentoring is long term and relationship focused.

Our beliefs are a very powerful thing. Think about the last time you were feeling discouraged; what were you saying to and about yourself? How did these thoughts impact your performance? What was the outcome?

What we are talking about here is called self-efficacy. Self-efficacy is the extent or strength of one's belief in one's own ability to complete tasks and reach goals. Self-efficacy impacts a person's ability to exercise influence over events that affect their life. People who experience high levels of self-efficacy think, feel, and act differently than people who have an inward sense of low self-efficacy. They remain calmer under stress, are more likely to perceive threatening situations as opportunity, and remain task-oriented in the face of challenges.

Coaching and mentoring go a long way in building as well as preventing a drop in a person's self-efficacy.

Fact: Self-efficacy has a greater impact on a person's success than I.Q.

Empower:

The first step in creating that win-win solution, as we discussed earlier, is by empowering your people to make decisions based on the situation at hand. Avoid treating every customer and every situation the same by hiding behind policy. When one of your people makes a decision in response to a customer's request, you must be prepared to back that decision and the representative to the wall, even if they make the wrong decision while serving the customer. Yes, even if they make the wrong decision.

Why is this important? When we empower people to make decisions, we must trust them. Let it be understood mistakes will be made. Mistakes are okay. Mistakes create learning opportunities. At Leader Within Us, we call this failing forward.

One of my favorite stories about failing forward comes from Thomas Edison. Upon the announcement of his success at inventing the light bulb, eager and excited reporters were firing question after question at the inventor. One of these reporters, in a very bold move, asked Edison…

"Mr. Edison, tell us about the 10,000 failures you had along the way."

Edison, wittily replied, "I have not failed. I've just found 10,000 ways that won't work."

Edison had the right idea, failure does not exist as long as we learn and apply forward. The moment we make our people wrong for the decision they make, we disempower them.

When people feel disempowered they become overly reliant on the supervisor; they become less engaged; they stop stretching and growing; they become "just a number" instead of an advocate for the company and the customer.

Making others wrong is leading in the opposite direction of creating a win-win solution.

I want to be clear. I am not suggesting every time some one makes a mistake we give them a sucker or a cookie. What I am suggesting is to direct attention to what they did right in order to encourage this behavior.

For corrective measures use open ended questions and coaching to identify and correct performance gaps. If further action is required, connect them with a mentor who excels in this area.

Measure:

Feedback is one of the most critical tools we have in our toolbox. I think most of you will agree with me on this. You can see this in the fact that organizations spend billions of dollars on satisfaction surveys internally and externally. I highly recommend asking for feedback on a regular basis - make it part of your culture.

One area that we fall short in is providing useful self-feedback. I say useful, because most of us are highly skilled at being self-critical and negative. This only breeds discouragement. What I am talking about is honest, specific, useful feedback by your own hands, not relying on someone else to place value for us.

Here is a model I use:

At the beginning of each day, put into practice a self-feedback process for each of your team. It consists of three questions:

- What am I setting out to do?
- What did I actually do?
- What was the outcome?

At the beginning of the day (call, interaction, etc.), answer the first question.

At the end of your day (call, interaction, etc.), answer the second and third questions.

From there ask yourself additional questions that fit this situation.

Examples might be:

- Did I get the outcome I intended? Why or why not?
- Is the customer fully satisfied with the outcome? Why or why not?
- What went well? Why?
- What can I do differently next time?
- Do I need additional training?
- What am I missing?

As I mentioned earlier, feedback is one of the most important, yet one of the most under utilized tools we have at our disposal. The following will help you be more successful with the feedback tool.

There are four basic types of feedback to be aware of:

- None   (the most common)
- Negative (the most abused)
- Positive   (the least effective)
- Specific   (the most helpful)

Guidelines to giving and receiving feedback:

- Feedback is information – nothing more, nothing less
- Feedback is never personal
- When giving feedback it's critical that it is timely (ASAP), specific, and valid
- Feedback will never be used to attack or make wrong
- Feedback will always be about the job or action, never the individual
- Feedback is about growth

Final Thoughts:

When we take the time, energy and effort to create other leaders, we make a greater impact on our world, our business and our personal lives. When we create leaders, they in turn create more leaders.

When we create followers…well, you know where this going.

The world doesn't need more followers.

When we create leaders of customer service excellence, we create advocates for greatness who will settle for nothing less.

Why settle for mediocrity?

David Erwin is a cultural anthropologist and storyteller with creative vision and a passion for delivering engaging training, coaching and speaking experiences.

He creates and delivers consistent and unique training ideas and products through data-driven insights, tactical execution and measurable results.

For over two decades he has been the Leader and all around Visionary of Leader Within Us, providing experience-based training and coaching for companies both large and small.

He has collaborated with and served organizations across major industries including, yet not limited to: High Tech, Medical, Airlines, Oil & Gas, Military and Financial Services in more than twenty-five countries and to hundreds of thousands of satisfied participants.

He is from Grand Prairie, Texas and currently resides in Tucson, Arizona. He is an adventurer, photographer, author, and globetrotter; he is profoundly curious about culture and has a deep love of people; his greatest passion is helping others move beyond their limiting beliefs into their limitless potential.

You can reach David at www.leaderwithin.us.

6 COMMUNICATION BY DESIGN
AUTHOR: CHAD FROESCHKE

I was one of the lucky few graduates to land a job right out of college. I remember my professor telling us "most graphic designers who don't find a job within 2 years after graduating rarely stay in their field of profession". So during the summer break between my sophomore and junior years I was accepted as an intern at one of the larger design firms in town.

I worked as much as I could - beyond my nine credit hours a week. I tried to immerse myself in all aspects of working at a design firm. From learning the computer (which wasn't available at my college until the semester I left), understanding the design and print lingo, requesting printing bids, creating estimates and actually meeting with clients.

I quickly understood that listening and communicating with clients is as, if not more, important than designing a marketing piece for them. I also realized that there is an "ideal evolution" in client relationships.

From the nervousness of the first introductory meeting, to setting the right tone in your voice, listening carefully to what your client's needs are, offering advice, and showing absolute support for your client's endeavors, I need to make sure my client understands and feels like they are part of a team whose sole purpose is to help make their business a success. And along this evolution client confidence builds, trust is gained and friendships grow. Your client becomes a part of your professional family and you build on this evolving relationship to help them succeed.

I also learned and experienced early on in my career that the "ideal evolution" in a client relationship can sadly and abruptly end. I began to realize the number one implication in the demise of client relationships is the lack of communication.

After eight years of learning the good and the bad, I decided to become my own boss and run a business – my business – the way I thought it should be run. The way my clients would want my business to be run. And I wanted to share with you some ideas and experiences in communication that I have learned and continue to implement in my business, for myself, and for my clients.

"Do what you say and say how you're going to do it"

One of the fastest ways to lose a client's trust and confidence is by breaking your own promises. This can take many forms such as a scheduled phone call, a meeting, work deadlines, and budgets. But the most frequent complaint new clients have expressed to me have been situations when their previous vendors fail to communicate deadlines and their work process.

When I'm meeting with a client (new or existing) it's essential that we create a timeline *together* for a project. Create your own personal "value stream" that illustrates - from beginning to end – your work process and all the steps that will occur. I discuss with my client when each milestone should occur, when deliverables are due (for both of us), and most importantly, we discuss the consequences of not meeting those milestones. For instance, if you and your client determine a certain project will take three weeks to complete and the first set of deliverables due from your client arrive a week late, then it should be understood that the project will now take four weeks to complete instead of three.

Life happens, but communicating with your clients of the shared responsibilities engages them in the ownership of the process. Your client understands they are part of the team and the team cannot function without everyone on board sharing the same goals and objectives. Creating a value stream with clients softens those awkward conversations when a project may not be delivered at a specific date.

Of course, not every project requires a meeting to discuss and write down value stream. Some projects will have a very short turnaround but the principles of timelines and deliverables should still be adhered to. It just makes common sense that if you accept a project – no matter what the turnaround – that you have the integrity and do what you say and say how you're going to do it.

"Listen, Collaborate, and Celebrate"

Everyone can "hear" a conversation but the key element when meeting with a client is to "listen". Listen for keywords that stand out in your meetings and direct your questions around those keywords to obtain more specific information; observe their emotions when talking about goals and obstacles and find ways to relate to them in your conversation.

One of the most challenging yet rewarding experiences I've had with a client was during our "Discover and Define" sessions for a new online business they were launching.

Discover and Define are two of the four phases in my value stream (followed by "Design and Development") that I introduce to my clients when presenting and developing web designs. In the Discover phase we collaborate together in several meeting to discuss the big-picture process. What are my client's goals and desired outcomes? What is important to them and *their* customers? And how does my client want their customers to experience *their* product? The Define phase is really putting pencil to paper (or in this instance a 4x8 dry-erase board). Together as a team we begin to create a "wireframe" or blueprint of the website. We discuss every page of the site, what information is given and why, how do the pages interact with each other and what the experience should be like for their customer.

My client is an industry leader in their field. They're incredibly talented and innovative and they see the big picture. Their goal was to transform their industry with an online service designed around how their customers would like to be treated. More efficient, more comprehensive, and consumer based. But it was the Define phase that was truly an experience in collaboration and teamwork. It was the minutia of the "Define" phase that evolved the "client relationship". What started out as a fairly straight-forward website estimated at 20 pages targeted to a single target audience evolved into a robust, comprehensive and innovative 180 page website designed and developed for three target audiences identified in the "Discover" phase. The goal was always the same, to create an "online service designed around how their customers would like to be treated", but the target audience evolved.

Over the next year, numerous meetings were held and thousands of questions were asked. As a team we experienced the full range of emotions together: laughter, frustration, fear, excitement, doubt, and confidence. During our meetings we developed a "code word" to use when a team-member would begin discussing unrelated topics or would tangent into topics already discussed and defined. We called this "code word" a "Hotdog". It was a great way to politely and humorously diffuse the tensions of frustration and confusion and at the same time make fun of ourselves – we're only human after all.

It's important to realize that your client knows their business better than you do. Understand that your role in collaboration is to enhance the future growth of *their* business – not yours. Make them a part of the team; cultivate the growth that helps them succeed and be open to all ideas when discussing strategy.

Our value stream changed significantly but eventually my client's goals came to fruition and their dream to set a new standard in the industry became a reality.

Before my clients website went "live" they hosted a launch party to give thanks to everyone that was involved: employees, investors, programmers, family and friends.

My client surprised many of us with awards of appreciation and I received the "Hotdog" award for my role in helping their dream become a reality!

My client's business is growing rapidly and I could not be more proud and excited for them. I'm grateful for the opportunity to have this "ideal evolution" in my client relationship. They're still my client and most importantly they are my friend.

My "Hotdog" award sits among my design and adverting awards in my conference room for all my clients to see. And when they ask the meaning of the award I proudly communicate my story.

Mr. Froeschke owns and operates WhiteSpace Design where he partners with both local businesses and national companies to help them communicate their brand vision through a creative and effective graphic design solution that's uniquely their own.

Since 2002, Mr. Froeschke has won over 60 awards for his creative design work. He is past President of both the Tucson GLBT Chamber of Commerce, Dynamic Connections Networking Group, and a member of the Tucson Marketing Pros and the Advertising Federation of Tucson. He has donated his time and talents to several non-profit organizations throughout the United States.

"Our goal is to always exceed our client's expectations. With years of experience working with companies both big and small, we aim to devise a visual style that sets you apart from the pack. Our extensive services are designed to help you grow your brand through innovative Design Consultation, Marketing Consultation and Conceptual Development. At WhiteSpace, we pride ourselves on creating award-winning designs, over multiple platforms and diverse environments with impact, flexibility and powerful results for your business."

www.whitespacedesigns.net

www.facebook.com/whitespacedesigns

7 HAPPY EMPLOYEES, HAPPY CUSTOMERS
AUTHOR: PAM FURLONG

Happy, successful employees take amazing care of your customers!

When your company provides a service or a product there should be 3 focal points.
1 Quality of product or service
2 Customer service
3 Fair pricing

Offering great customer service requires a well trained team with a great attitude. In other words, the kind of team your competitors would love to steal from you. To prevent that, we created pay scales based on skill levels that our team members could achieve. Creating this atmosphere allowed our team members to be challenged, and self promote by taking charge of their own advancement and future. Our team helped one another learn new skills and increase their earnings. We paid a bonus to the whole team if we exceeded our sales budget. Our press operators and graphic designers were paid on the amount of work they could produce daily verses an hourly fee. When I hired I looked for people that were likable, cheerful, helpful, positive and had a great interest to grow and evolve in our industry. Some people are looking for a job and any job will do, but I wanted people who desired a career, not just a job. The bonus to all this was they took amazing care of our customers and we won 1st, 2nd, and 3rd place in a mystery shopper contest for customer service among the 15 Tucson Alphagraphics print shops.

We not only wanted our employees to know the business, we wanted them to have fun things to look forward to, such as:

- Paid vacation, plus a day off for their birthday.
- Annual company campout with their families.
- Weekend at the lake with cookout and water skiing.
- Annual Holiday Party with Santa and Mrs. Claus and gifts for the children.
- We gave awards voted on by the team for: Most valuable player, rookie of the year, best cheerleader and team manager of the year. The award was a framed cartoon character drawn of the team member including the award title printed on it. We announced and presented these at the annual Holiday Party.
- An inside lunch/break room with a dining table, chairs, refrigerator, microwave, sofa and TV.
- An outside lunch/break area.
- Holiday gifts.

Let me tell you about the amazing things my team did for me and our customers.

We started out as a team of 7 and grew to a team of 37.

98% of our orders were delivered on time as promised, with 45% of those being delivered early. That is amazing in an industry that is known for being late.

When customers asked for a rush order, we would work through the night to accommodate them. We pulled many all nighters. We eventually added a night shift, because we became known for pulling people out of binds.

One of my former team members started working for a law firm and brought us their business, which was significant.

On occasion, a customer would knock on our door after we had closed and our team would always open the door and serve them. There is nothing worse than racing across town and arriving to locked doors a few minutes after closing.

Team members would carry jobs out to customer's cars.

They would give customers a tour of the shop and introduce them to the team behind the scene.

One time a customer (approx 75 years old) called me and said she was so touched and wanted me to know that one of our team members called her to make sure she was alright, since he hadn't seen her lately.

I would often hear them offering customers water, especially in the summer.

The sales team delivered Valentines, Halloween, and other Holiday treats to our customers.

Quotes were given to the customer while they were on the phone or at the front counter. We won more jobs by getting quotes out fast. I can tell you that is not the norm. There are some exceptions and I prefer working with those suppliers who work with a sense of urgency.

We included surveys with every order and we shared them with all the team when they were positive. When we received concerns, we saw it as a gift and opportunity to make it right. It also let us know where we needed to focus training. If a customer shared a concern with us, I would personally call them to ask how I could make it right for them. Most often they just wanted to let you know. Don't guess what will make it right, ask them. Why guess when you can know.

Usually 80% of your business comes from 20% of your customers. We knew our 20% and worked hard to build great relationships with them. The team would let me know when one of them came into the store, so I could say hello and check in with them. We knew them by name. If we knew their birthdays, we would send them a card. We made it a point to know their business anniversary and send them a rose for every year they were in business. Customers were amazed that we remembered.

If we got invited to a business open house, we would take a plant. Once a customer invited me in to see how much the plant had grown. I was amazed that she remembered who had given her the plant.

Customers would bring us gifts all the time to say thank you for helping them out. One time, a retiring gentleman, gave all his beautiful ties to one of my new managers.

Avoid the word no and offer options. Customers sometimes don't know they have other options. Example: Rather than telling a customer we could not have 500 printed white sheets with red ink in 10 minutes, we would say "I can have that for you later tomorrow or we could copy 500 sheets of red paper with black in the next 10 minutes. Would that work?"

Always be helpful. Lost people would come in to the shop and ask for directions. We would call where they were going and get turn by turn directions for them. That was before on-line navigation. Now we would print a map for them or set up their GPS on their smart phone.

In closing I want to remind you that you're the expert in your customer's eyes. When someone asks you a question, they don't know what they don't know and that is why they are looking to you in the first place. Help them get pointed in the right direction, so they can accomplish what they set out to do. Don't be another road block. Help them to at least get to the next step. Help them get closer to the solution. One of my favorite sayings is "How do you eat an elephant? One bite at a time." Be helpful and think how you can help them move towards a solution.

Take care of your team and they will take care of your customers!

Pam is an Arizona native, born in Phoenix, raised in Tucson and continues to make it her home.

In 1976 Pam worked part time at a corporate Alphagraphics print shop while she was attending college. From 1981 to 2000 Pam was president of Furlong Inc. and owned 5 Alphagraphics shops in Tucson. Furlong Inc. was a family affair.

In 2007 Pam started Tucson Marketing Tools with 4 rules: No equipment, no employees, no bricks and mortar and could be managed from anywhere with the help of the internet. Tucson Marketing Tools offers: Printing, email marketing and promotional items.

Pam is master certified by Constant Contact to teach their online marketing program called *Toolkit* including the following tools: Email marketing, survey, event registration, promotions, Facebook fans and autoresponders.

Pam Furlong – Tucson Marketing Tools

520-742-2498 - Pam@tucsonmarketingtools.com

www.tucsonmarketingtools.com

8 CREATING AN EXTRAORDINARY CUSTOMER EXPERIENCE FROM THE INSIDE OUT
AUTHOR: MJ JENSEN

A business owner I know wanted me to help her create a complete advertising campaign using money she was going to borrow from the SBA (Small Business Administration). I about fell off my chair! It wasn't because of the money she was going to borrow for the advertising. It was because I knew that she had not addressed her internal customers first.

All the advertising, marketing, promotions, and social media in the world will NOT overcome the pitfalls of not creating an extraordinary "internal" customer experience first.

Who is your "internal" customer?

Your "internal" customers are your employees, your vendors, your sphere of influence (friends, family, and associates) and your existing customers.

Business owners forget sometimes that it's the people closest to you that have the most influence over the success (or lack of) of your business.

When was the last time that you were in contact with all of the above about updates in your business? By the way, this is NOT about selling to them. This is about building your relationships with them.

Let's start with your existing customers.

These are your potential "Raving Fans". They are the ones that have already experienced your product or service. What would they say about that experience? If you're not sure, then ask them. Send out an online survey and ask questions that will draw out their REAL feelings. Make it confidential so they will be honest in their feedback. I have filled out dozens of online surveys about my own personal experiences with businesses. The ones that I take the time to fill out are simple, easy and straightforward. I like to use Survey Money, but there other equally effective and free surveys to use. If you tie an incentive to the completed form and they have to give their name, don't expect that you will gain truthful and honest feedback. I just spent the weekend at a local resort and for the most part it was amazing. However, there was one BIG issue. Our hot water in the shower did NOT work. By the time we discovered the situation, we were ready to check out. The resort sent me an online survey and in that format I was able to inform them of the problem. Do you think they appreciated knowing there was a problem? I trust that they did appreciate knowing. I also appreciated the opportunity to inform them in a non-confrontational way.

Once you have feedback then it's time to repair, correct and solve the problems. I look at this as another opportunity to communicate with your existing customers about your plans on improving their experience with you. It's not enough to make the changes or corrections and then not inform them.

You can use a number of different tools to keep in communication with your "internal" customer. Email marketing is an effective tool since most of us use our emails to do online ordering. I do know that more and more people are not checking email. So what do you do if you cannot reach them via email? Try using an actual person to follow up.

One of my clients is a top automotive repair and maintenance facility and they call all customers after a visit to their locations. This is an "Old School" process that I believe still works today. It brings that personalized approach in a world where technology has taken over.

Believe it or not, snail mail still works, too. We use personalized cards like Send Out Cards to make that message memorable.

What this tells you is no one thing works for everyone. Integrate a number of ways of communicating with your existing customers and they will reward you for it by referring more business to you.

And that brings me to another pet peeve of mine. Asking for referrals!

I see this all the time in certain industries like Real Estate, Mortgage Lending, Insurance and other service related businesses. They use slogans like "I LOVE Referrals". REALLY??? Who doesn't love referrals? That doesn't encourage me to hand over my precious sphere of influence to a person or business that does not earn it. I give referrals because the business is extraordinary! I reward businesses with my referrals because they have gone above and beyond my expectation of exceptional service. The business that gains my referrals has surprised me with an extraordinary experience.

When I receive referrals from my sphere of influence, I keep them informed of the progress of the connection. If it turns into business, I invite my referring partner to lunch. It gives us a chance to get to know each other on a deeper level and I can discover how I can be a referral source for them. I sometimes send small thank you gifts and a thank you note. This is how I have been able to encourage many referrals from the same people. They aren't referring to me because I send them a gift. They keep referring business to me because I take the time to acknowledge them and thank them for their support.

I refer a LOT of business to other businesses. I rarely get thanked and even acknowledged for the referral. Don't be that business. Take time to honor the referral sources that support you. You will never have to ask for a referral again.

In all the years I have been a marketing advisor I have yet to see things break down with customers if there is more than enough of the right communication. Things break down when there is not enough or no communication. The one major complaint I hear from people about their unsatisfactory experiences with businesses is that the business did NOT keep in contact with them. It is NOT the customers' responsibility to communicate with the business. It is the business' responsibility to stay in communication with the customer/client. I listen to excuses that some businesses make when a customer has a complaint and one of the things that does come up is, "They didn't tell me there was a problem." That tells me the business has not taken responsibility for staying in contact with their customers/clients.

The industries that I have observed that are generally the worst at follow up and communication are contractors, realtors, cable companies, landscaping companies, doctor's offices, Contact Us online forms (any industry), restaurants, and this is just to name a few. The businesses that I personally refer business to in these industries are at the top of the game when it comes to follow up and communication.

There are so many tools to use to stay in contact with customers/clients. It is a non-negotiable process in your business. My hair salon, dentist and my acupuncture office all have systems that remind me of my appointments via email and by text. I don't miss any of those appointments because they have made it easy for me to remember. And it has cut down on no-shows for all three businesses.

Before my clients can ask, "I wonder what MJ is doing on our marketing?", I have already been in frequent contact via email, phone call, text or Facebook message to give them updates. The frequency depends on the customer and the process. Some customers expect daily check in. Some clients may not need to hear from you more than once a week. If you're not sure what they expect, ask them what works best and what communication tool they prefer. Do not treat all of your customers the same when it comes to communication and follow up. Everyone will have a unique and different expectation of "what is enough". In my initial consultation and intake with a client, I review what the best way to stay in contact and what is a reasonable amount of contact with them.

That brings me to the follow up process.

We strive to follow up 100% of the time on everything. Is that easy? Nope! It is what we hang our marketing hats on though. It's what sets IdeaMagic visionary marketing & social media apart from the other marketing companies out there. Clients, our sphere of influence and the general community know that if I say I will do something, it gets done – on time. And I make sure the person I have made that promise to is aware that it has been completed. The reason why I'm mentioning this here is that I see a lack of 100% Follow Up and Follow Through everywhere I go. People make promises and then do not follow through. This is one of those extraordinary customer experiences that is so easy to implement. It doesn't cost money. And it makes a huge impact on the customers and clients you serve. If you can't keep your promise, do not make the promise. I'm not clear why this is an issue for some folks. Maybe it's because they want to over promise and under deliver. We prefer to over promise and over deliver. Yes you read that right. We over promise and we over deliver. If you are looking to be at the top of the game in your industry – strive for 100% Follow Up and Follow Through!

Now let's go back to creating an exceptional experience for your employees.

Actually, I would like to start with establishing your company culture and the U.S.P. (Unique Selling Position) of your company. This sets the tone for recruiting and retaining the Ideal Employee in your company. How does this relate to "Creating an Extraordinary Customer Experience? Because you are only as good (or bad) as your best or worst employee. All it takes is one bad apple in the apple cart to ruin the entire bunch. And believe me, I've seen it happen more times than I care to admit. It is our responsibility to educate, nurture and lead our TEAM to greatness. It is their responsibility to be open, receptive, willing to change and learn. If you are hiring the right people for your company culture, your extraordinary customer experiences will soar. Your business will increase and your profitability will increase. If you are losing customers, your business is not growing, and if you are seeing more negative online reviews, it's time to take stock and remove the bad apples.

The Ideal Employee will see your vision of your company culture and embrace the vision. The Ideal Employee will be empowered to make the right decisions for the customer - every time.

Take Nordstrom for example. They are legendary in providing an extraordinary customer experience. The people on the sales floor know what they need to do to WOW the customer that walks through their doors. Nordstrom became the benchmark for all fine retailers around the world. It wasn't just about the products. It was about the experience and the feeling that was created for each and every customer.

So, you've hired the Ideal Employee; now what do you do to

keep them? I look at how great companies around the country have created a company culture where the employees have fun, are appreciated and want to stick around. It's not that difficult to create that kind of place to work. When was the last time you had a company party to celebrate your successes? I recommend that my clients host a celebratory "party" every Friday. You can use it as a time to train and educate, too. The premise is to bring your TEAM together and just have fun. How does this relate to creating an extraordinary customer experience? Remember in the first part of this chapter I talked about who is your "internal customer"? Your Ideal Employees are THE most important customer you serve. Notice I mention "Ideal Employees" again. If you don't believe you have the Ideal Employees in your company, now is the time to change.

Creating a culture of Ideal Employees is also about communication and 100% Follow Up and Follow Through. It means sitting down with all of them a minimum of twice a year. Not just a review, but a chance to get feedback on how they believe things are going in their part of the company and then following up to make sure that their reasonable requests are being implemented. Not all employee requests are reasonable and I understand that, but for the most part, I believe people that are truly invested in the company and the customers will be reasonable in their requests.

If you've ever watched **_Undercover Boss_** on TV, this is a series that shows CEOs going undercover and in disguise to see what's REALLY going on in their company. Many times the CEO would see how passionate and caring the employees are, but no one had ever acknowledged their commitment and loyalty. The CEO comes out without the disguise and offers the employees amazing gifts and incentives for their loyalty. Many times the entire company morale changed for the better because of what the Leader did to honor some of the employees.

Employees are like children in many ways. If you nurture them, guide them, communicate effectively, be a Boss that walks the talk when it comes to integrity and creating an extraordinary customer experience, your "children" will thrive! And they will go out of their way to nurture, educate and communicate effectively with the customers and clients.

Do you see how this trickle UP effect is working? The Ideal Employee REALLY wants to do the right thing not only for the company, but for the customers, too.

The Ideal Employees are the foundation of an extraordinary customer experience. Make sure your foundation is solid, strong and will last a long time.

Let's talk about how to engage your sphere of influence.

Your spheres of influence are all of the people that may have a personal connection to you, but have no idea what you do or how to help you. The important thing to note is that we are NOT selling to them. We want to include them. Include them in company gatherings and announcements of upcoming changes and opportunities. Include them on press releases, newsletters and any awards events. You will be amazed at how many people in your sphere of influence are thrilled to be included and are honored to refer more business to you and your company. These are the people that are REALLY invested in your success and will bend over backwards to make sure that their sphere of influence knows what you do and who you are. Let's make sure we do NOT take them for granted. They are a critical component in the growth and success of creating an exceptional customer experience.

So you've read my philosophy about where to begin in creating an extraordinary customer experience. It may seem a little unusual and maybe not what you expected, but it's my job to shake your world up and bring ideas that will excite, ignite, and attract business to your business.

I know that if you are willing to put in the time and effort to implementing all of the information in this chapter, your business will increase and you will have more fun. Because isn't that what this is all about?

MJ Jensen is the Chief Idea Officer for Tucson based company called IdeaMagic visionary marketing & social media. She also runs the dynamic and successful group called Tucson Marketing Professionals. MJ's passion is helping small businesses find affordable and creative solutions to all of their marketing and social media. MJ's mission is to help herself and others find success personally, professionally and spiritually. MJ along with her husband, Charley, love to kayak, go camping and are Denver Broncos fanatics.

MJ Jensen, Chief Idea Officer

IdeaMagic visionary marketing & social media

The "Queen" of Tucson Marketing Professionals

You can reach MJ at:

www.IdeaMagic.com

Facebook – IdeaMagic

Facebook – Tucson Marketing Professionals

9 PLATINUM CUSTOMER SERVICE IS FOUND IN OUR VALUES
AUTHOR: DIANE KEPHART

"When your values are clear to you, making decisions becomes easier."

- Roy E. Disney

Someone said to me the other day that they were surprised how quickly I was able to make decisions. I told them it was because I had clear values. And I filter all decisions through these values.

As an Air Force veteran, I realize that the three Air Force core values that I modeled as a military officer continue to guide the way I offer my clients platinum customer service today.

These are: Integrity first, service before self, and excellence in all that we do.

"To give real service you must add something which cannot be bought or measured with money, and that is sincerity and integrity."

- Douglas Adams

INTEGRITY FIRST

As a foundation of this platinum service, we begin with integrity. All other values build upon this one. It's being honest with others as well as with yourself, and doing what's right at all times - even when no one is looking - regardless of the circumstances. It is an attitude of no compromise when it comes to integrity. Period.

"Real integrity is doing the right thing, knowing that nobody's going to know whether you did it or not."

- Oprah Winfrey

"What is the right thing to do?"

This question should guide all of our daily decisions and actions. Often, the easiest or most convenient thing isn't the right thing. And in the short-term, doing what is easy may even cause us great personal gain. But in the long run, doing what is right, refusing to compromise our integrity, will build lasting customer relationships.

When you are known for being a person of integrity, it builds trust. Our word MUST be our bond. If you make an appointment, show up. If you say you will do something, do it. No excuses. Period. People know that if I commit to be somewhere or to finish a task, they can count on me to follow through. This is being a person of your word and a person of integrity. What is your reputation among those you know and serve?

When I served as a manager for a national quick-service restaurant, I was amazed how many potential employees would commit to come to an interview or be hired and say they would show up for work, but then didn't follow through on their word.

When one of my clients calls me, I ensure I follow through on what I have told them I will do for them or that I am early if I have promised to meet with them. If this ever becomes impossible, due to a family emergency or something outside of my control, I call them immediately. Another part of modeling integrity is showing up on time or early. This shows you value the other person and his or her time.

Living with integrity includes an attitude of under promising, allowing our service providers to over-deliver. Could I make more sales if I promised prospective customers that we would do things for them that I know are not covered in their plan? Probably. But is that acting with integrity?. No. And over time, my business and relationships are much stronger when I don't go for the easy sale, but for what is right. Integrity first - an Air Force value and critical foundation of platinum service.

"I don't know what your destiny will be, but one thing I know: the only ones among you who will be really happy are those who have sought and found how to serve."

— Albert Schweitzer

SERVICE BEFORE SELF

Platinum customer service requires an attitude of service before self. Putting our needs secondary to the needs of our customers may require personal sacrifice at times. But it is also one of the strongest ways to build great client loyalty and trust. Our being inconvenienced at times allows us to do what is most convenient for those we have committed to serve.

Since I work in the areas of identity-theft and legal protection, I have frequent opportunities to show my clients service before self. One recent example was a panicked phone call I received from a client. He had filed his taxes and found out that someone had already filed under his social security number. He felt violated, stressed, worried. I had a split-second decision to make. The easy thing would have been to give him the toll-free number to call one of our licensed private investigators to help him through the situation. But the better choice was for me to make the call with him on the phone, explain the situation, introduce him, then let the licensed private investigator take over the call and assist him.

Which took more time? The second choice. Which made my client feel valued as a member and not just a number? The second choice. This was also the right decision and allowed me to show him by my actions that I was there to serve him after the sale.

Another recent example was a client and entrepreneur who has our small business plan. He needed a contract reviewed, but it had to be signed before our usual 3-day turn around period in document reviews. We were able to call the law firm, explain the urgency, and they bumped his request up in priority allowing him to meet the deadline for signing.

"How May I Help?"

This one question shows people that you are more concerned about them than you are about yourself or making a "sale." It makes them feel valued, important, and shows you really care.

Platinum customer service focuses on building relationships and keeping great clients who become friends.

"People of excellence go the extra mile to do what's right."

— Joel Osteen

Think about times in your life when you have experienced great customer service. Were you made to feel extremely valued, that your experience was the most important? What stood out to you in your memory of that experience?

"Though my work may be menial, though my contribution may be small, I can perform it with dignity and offer it with unselfishness. My talents may not be great, but I can use them to bless the lives of others.... The goodness of the world in which we live is the accumulated goodness of many small and seemingly inconsequential acts."

— Gordon B. Hinckley

Did a hotel employee make your stay celebrating a special event even more meaningful by doing the little, unexpected things?

I experienced this recently on my youngest daughter's 18th birthday. I had bought a night's stay at a local hotel at a charity auction. When I called the hotel to make a reservation, I casually mentioned it was going to be a special way of celebrating her birthday since her dad had passed of cancer 2 1/2 years prior to that day.

Without my request or knowledge, the hotel staff decorated the room with a birthday banner, balloons, and chocolates. These all made her feel special and required extra effort on the staff's part. They sacrificed time and energy for us. But how many people do you think have heard me tell that story and recommend that hotel?

Platinum customer service causes our customers to brag about us to others.

It is so gratifying when one of my clients calls me, often in tears, to share a story of how she has used our service and has been able to resolve a challenge in which she previously saw no hope.

For example, I have a client whose husband has a debilitating illness so he spends most of his day in a recliner. The recliner, although under warranty, broke. So she called the furniture store and they promised her a part within two weeks to fix it. Two weeks later, they told her it would take a month. And then they called and said it would be up to six months IF they could get the part. This would push it beyond the warranty period. Since he was uncomfortable, she was stressed. But as my member, I was able to help her call our dedicated provider law firm. Our attorney listened to her situation, wrote a letter on her behalf to the furniture store, mailed it, and she called me in tears the next week. She had just received a call from the manager of the store. He said she could choose any recliner in stock, they would scotchguard it for free, deliver it for free the next day, and pick up the broken one. She was relieved, grateful, and hopeful.

It was also extremely gratifying to have that same client refer a member of her family and a friend to me because she trusts me to show them the same level of service she has received from me and from our service providers.

When I meet with a potential client, I ask questions to learn about them, their business, their family, and any challenges they may be facing. Then I ask, "How may I help you?"

When an existing client reaches out to me with a situation, I ask, "How may I help?" This attitude of service before self is one of the key values in our U.S. Air Force. As a veteran, I have seen this attitude permeate the actions of our Airmen.

But the attitude of Service Before Self is refreshing in customer service as well.

"Perfection is not attainable, but if we chase perfection we can catch excellence."

- Vince Lombardi

EXCELLENCE IN ALL THAT WE DO

Our clients and referring partners have entrusted us to serve their needs or to serve their referrals. Doing the very best we can is not just a professional obligation, but it is also a moral one. When we exhibit excellence, we build trust and set the standard for others to respect and follow.

Are you known as a person of excellence? Do you compromise in what you give your customers or do you strive to set the standard of excellence in every interaction, every presentation that you do?

"If you are going to achieve excellence in big things, you develop the habit in little matters. Excellence is not an exception, it is a prevailing attitude."

- Colin Powell

Excellence is not easy. It is an attitude of continuous self-improvement, knowing that we can always get better and learn from others.

I've told my children that we can learn from everyone we meet. From some, we learn how to live our lives and how to conduct ourselves to become better. From others, we learn how not to be.

 Excellence also means anticipating our clients' needs. Is serving them our primary focus? At the end of the day, are we proud of the job we did? At the end of the month, did we work hard to accomplish our goals and to finish strong? Or did we compromise and settle for less than our best effort? Excellence in all that we do requires a daily focus, a daily effort to accept nothing less than our best.

"Be a yardstick of quality. Some people aren't used to an environment where excellence is expected."

- Steve Jobs

I had a supervisor who said something 20 years ago that still impacts me today. "If I see something wrong and say nothing about it, I have just set a new standard of acceptability." Let us ensure we are setting the standard of excellence and nothing less as we strive to provide platinum customer service.

Excellence has its rewards. I have a client who has used our service and is very satisfied and happy with his membership. He referred me to a company with 20 employees. Through our voluntary employee benefits division, I was able to share our membership with the employees during a morning meeting and 60% chose to enroll as members that day through payroll deduction. I would not have been able to meet and now serve these members had I been satisfied with mediocrity when serving my client. Through excellent service, we built trust and he has become a wonderful referring partner.

Integrity first, service before self, and excellence in all things we do. Think about these core values as our GPS guiding our actions and decisions in our professional and personal life. Then, and only then, we will be able to create a habit of platinum customer service that our clients will value and respect.

Diane M. Kephart, a former US Air Force officer (and die-hard Buckeye fan) has lived in Ohio, Florida, Texas, Japan, Colorado, and Arizona. She and her late husband, also a veteran, have a son and two daughters who are working to "finish strong" in their high school, college, and careers. Her heart is with military families as she understands and has experienced the unique challenges they face. She believes we all go through difficulty so that we are able to help others facing the same. Diane is a small business and voluntary employee benefits specialist who has earned a company-paid BMW. She loves helping people daily by giving them hope through affordable access to legal advice and to identity-theft protection and restoration. She also enjoys empowering entrepreneurs who have big business problems, but small business budgets. She is blessed and will soon marry another LegalShield executive director and they will continue to serve others in everything they do in their lives together.

Diane M Kephart
LegalShield Independent Associate - Executive Director

www.dihelpspeople.com - 720-496-8277
www.livecompanyoverview.com/dmkephart

10 THE CUSTOMER EXPERIENCE
AUTHORS: RICK MOORE & KAREN CUNY BRADLEY

Our company, Moore Security Solutions, is a local, Tucson based Security Alarm and Video Surveillance Company. We are integrators who sell, service and install commercial and residential security alarms, video surveillance, access control, fleet GPS management systems and medical alert devices. We have been protecting southern Arizona for more than 16 years. We take the business of securing the community very seriously and provide not only great customer service but professional installation with secure and reliable monitoring. We have recently been bombarded by the larger companies such as Cox, AT&T and Verizon entering the security world. What they can provide is large scale advertising, which informs the public about the availability of their services. What they cannot provide is that personal touch. That company that goes the extra mile, is flexible, knows each and every one of their clients and truly cares about their safety. This is where we have the advantage. This is what separates our company from the huge players in the security industry.

In the world of mergers and acquisitions and companies growing into huge conglomerates, we are experiencing less and less of that personal touch when we purchase products and services. We have seen telephone answering systems be the norm where you have to go through a series of prompts to get the right person. These large companies make it harder and harder to find their phone numbers on their websites; instead resorting to the web for "customer service" and having the customer do everything by themselves. Sometimes they give you the option of using a chat box, email or a recording to get you your information. If you do finally get through, that person may be in India, you can hardly understand them and they can only help with very simple issues. While all this may be more efficient for the company providing it, as a consumer it can be very frustrating. Sometimes we just need to talk to someone in customer service, a real person, but after being transferred six times and put on "ignore" you end up irritated and angry. What this type of customer service from the big impersonal companies does is drive a wedge between themselves and their client. That client just so happens to be the one that is sending them money each and every month.

It is not just the ability to communicate easily by telephone the big companies are doing this with. This culture exists throughout their organizations. They have procedures and protocols and even if you attempt to escalate your problem up the corporate responsibility ladder, the people you are talking to have little to no authority to adjust the corporate rules. We recently had an issue with our cell phone bill. So we gave them a call, and after fifteen minutes on hold, we find out that our carrier does not send out detailed bills. We had tried to go onto the website to get the information, but we had to toggle back and forth between several pages for each line of information we had. It became so frustrating that we called to get a paper bill. To our ever lasting chagrin,they wanted to charge us $8.00 to send a detailed bill to our email! This is a company that we send several hundred dollars to each month! I was only asking for the detail on what I was paying as they didn't easily provide it with their regular billing. They are the same type of company that tells me in the beginning of my phone calls how "important" our call is to them. I think if it was important, as they say, they would not let us wait for 20 minutes before speaking to someone. Customer service is just not good customer service in many companies we all deal with everyday.

What this does for the small business owner is to provide an opportunity to give the customer what they need; a positive transaction, a personal feeling of concern for their needs and desires and some respect. Since the small business owner does not have the resources of the big corporations, the owners must provide that exceptional customer experience that the big boys are just not capable of making happen. This is the differentiator. This is our opportunity. This is where we can develop a relationship with the customer that is positive and desirable to both parties. At Moore Security Solutions, we strive to make the customers and clients know how important they are by answering the phones with a live person and communicating directly with them. We do not put people on hold, we do not have an overseas call center and we do really mean it when we say they are important to us. All of this matters and is an integral part of our company culture.

Although our company is a small business, we have developed a very positive company culture. Those in the office and in the field know that we strive to provide the best service and go above and beyond with our customers. Company culture starts at the top and trickles down via example and training. We work with our staff to understand that we are going to do what the customer wants and we are going to help them in any way we can. I recently had a call from a new client. She was very skittish about having a technician come in to install a security system and video surveillance cameras. Although we reassured her that our technician was qualified, trustworthy and personable, she still wanted the owner to come out that day. Not only did our owner go out to make our new client comfortable, she loved our technician. She called me later to ask me where he liked to eat as he went above and beyond and helped her with a problem she was having with her gate. She went out while he was still there and purchased a gift card for a restaurant because she knew he went the extra mile to help her in a totally unrelated problem. This is exactly the type of "customer experience" we want at Moore Security Solutions.

Most people in small business, the entrepreneurs of the world, will tell you they are different from their competitors by the customer service they provide. But, what exactly does that mean? Everyone can say that, but performing each and every time is not always an easy thing to do. We choose to not to call it customer service, but "the customer experience". Because that is truly what consumers want. They want to feel important and they want to have their "experience" with you be a positive one, whether it is by telephone or in person. When you go out to eat, if the food is good but the service terrible, you have had a bad experience and don't go back. Then you tell 10 friends about how terrible it was. Well the food wasn't bad but you had an expectation that you would be waited on in a timely and professional manner. You don't really go out to eat just for the food.

You go out to be waited on and you rely on your server for that great experience. Your expectations have not been met, your experience was a poor one and you won't go back. How much does that cost the company? There really isn't a way to measure that. In turn, how much does it profit if you have a good experience? You will return and you will tell your friends. In our business these are referrals and they are invaluable.

Below are some of the ways in which we provide our customers and clients with an excellent customer experience.

1. We answer the phones 24/7 with a live, friendly voice and regardless of the time, we try our very best to solve their concerns or answer their questions. In our industry, this task is often handled by a call center. That operator really has no idea how the company works. They can only take a message and have someone call you back, usually the next day. If your alarm is going off in the middle of the night and you are extremely upset , you want someone that can help you at that very moment. We know that is important.

2. If a call does go to voicemail, we try to return that call immediately. If for some reason, we can't, we strive for a return call no more than 2 hours after they have tried to contact us.

3. We take the time to listen to what their needs are and to ask a lot of questions. Whether they are on the phone with a problem, in the field with a technician, or even in the sales process we attempt to assess what they are really wanting in regards to the project at hand or service needed. So many companies will try to tell you what you need because they need to sign a contract. In our industry the big companies use several people in the process of gaining a new customer. They drop kids off in a neighborhood to knock on doors. Those kids make money based on the sales and upselling they do. They have no idea how it is installed and frankly don't care. This is someone you will never see again and will likely not be with the company in two months. Then they have someone come in to install the equipment this guy sold. These are usually done by a service company that they have no control over. We have seen some pretty awful installations by very incompetent people. This is your family or

business security; something that should be taken very seriously. The only people that you will deal with over the long term are the administrative people who don't know you from the thousands of other customers. There is nothing personal or warm about your dealings with them. And they are there to uphold the rules, regardless of what the sales person said or the installer did. Even when they are wrong and did terrible things to you by lying to you from the beginning, they will NOT let you out of your contract.

4. We truly care about each and every one of our customers and their continued business. We try to tell them that every chance we get. We tell them in the invoices we send quarterly, sometimes with a hand written note, sometimes in the newsletter and sometimes in a gift card just saying "Thank You". We have many customers who pay us each and every month and we truly appreciate that. When is the last time that your cable company or cell phone carrier sent you a handwritten note thanking you for your business? We know this is one of the ways to keep our customers loyal.

5. We follow through with each and every person, no matter how big or small their needs. This may be in servicing their account, making service appointments, or emailing them back answering a question or problem. We let them know when we have completed what they asked us to do so they are not left wondering if it was actually done. This gives them the reassurance that not only do we know what we are doing, but in the security industry it can be their safety we are compromising if something is not done.

6. We are flexible in all that we do. Although we have procedures, everyone's needs are different. We don't believe that one answer fits everyone's needs. We had an instance recently where we were installing GPS devices on a company's trucks. Our technicians don't start work until 8 am but the customer didn't want to take their trucks out of commission while the GPS was installed as it costs them time and money when their staff isn't working. We made special arrangements with one of our technicians to come in at 6:30 am for several days to get their trucks done at the beginning of their day, not ours. This was a commitment on our part and the part of

our technician to be accommodating to their needs. These things are about being flexible and doing what THEY want, regardless of the additional time and money it may cost us to do so.

7. We carefully screen our employees both in the field and in the office. Our technicians are in people's houses and businesses every day. We and our customers need to know they are trustworthy and honest, in addition to being competent and friendly. We do extensive background and drug testing and check references.

8. We do our own service work with our own employees. In addition to doing work for our customers, we also do work for some of the big security companies who farm out their service work. Not one of those companies has asked about whether we do background checks on our technicians. They really have no idea who we are sending to their customer's houses. We literally could hire someone off the street to do the service work for them and they would have no say. This is one of the many reasons to "Go Local" and use a company that has a true vested interest in your safety and security. You know that person is a company employee and has been background checked. In the security industry this is invaluable as that person often knows your codes and how to work your security system.

9. We send out newsletters and emails about new products, additional safety measures, safety tips and many ways to keep secure. This allows our clients to see the latest products and gives them a little more information that can help to keep them secure. It also keeps them in touch with what is happening at Moore Security Solutions.

10. We take responsibility for our mistakes. Mistakes will happen but it is important to admit to them and resolve them immediately. We always ask, "What would you like us to do?" This gives them power and lets us know their expectations. We can't always do what they want, but we always try to make accommodations for them in one way or another.

11. We have set procedures in place in both the office and the field. We use checklists to assure that all of the steps are followed with each and every person and nothing is forgotten. In the office we make sure their information is entered properly and then double checked once it is entered. For a new customer, this checklist goes as far as sending them a thank you note for choosing Moore Security Solutions as their security provider. In the field, we make sure that the technicians test the system to make sure it is working properly. They test signals with the monitoring station and check all batteries while they are there, regardless of the reason for the service call. This prevents problems in the future and reassures the customer that their system is working properly.

12. We have a referral program in place. We realize the true value of a referral. If someone is referred to us and they are already a customer we give them 3 free months of monitoring and send them a thank you note. If they are not a customer, we send a thank you note and a gift card. We realize that a referral is the ultimate form of trust as they are referring a friend or family member with the knowledge that we will take good care of them.

13. We are very good at giving that personal touch to everything we do. We feel it is important for our customers to know all of the people in the office as they will be dealing with all of us during their time with us. Often they have met the owner as he is the one who personally goes to their home to do a walkthrough. Then they meet the technicians, often for hours and hours at a time as they are doing the work, whether it is a 15 minute service call or a full two or three day video installation. But then we make sure they also meet (sometimes in person) the person who will be responsible for servicing their account. This is important as most often from that time forward that is who they will be talking to. We take the time to call them if they are a new customer and welcome them, make sure everything went well and let them know our names and that we are here to help them. Our customers really appreciate this extra touch.

14. We are honest and fair in each and every one of our dealings with our customers. When we give a bid, that is the bid. If it takes us

much longer than expected to do the job and none of it was their fault, we do not change the prices. A bid is a bid and that is what they will pay unless they change the plan that was proposed during the installation. We don't lie to our customers or potential customers to get the sales. Honesty and integrity are part of the customer experience and our company culture. We find that because we are knowledgeable, friendly and trustworthy, we will get the job. It is not always about the price. It is about value and providing that special customer experience.

15. We utilize social media to keep our customers informed and knowledgeable. We have Facebook, Twitter, Google +, Linked In, Pinterest and You Tube accounts that we post on regularly. We post information on products, specific safety tips and news we feel is relevant to our listeners. We have a You Tube Channel with videos on how to do things with your security panel such as bypassing a zone or adding a user. We understand that people like to be able to see a video on how to do something rather than be given the instructions. Social Media is growing and more and more people, especially young people, are utilizing it to find answers to their questions.

These are just some of the things we think are most important in creating and keeping our customers and in creating a positive customer experience. We strive to not just do our best, but to go above and beyond with everyone we come in contact with. This may be a customer, or it may just be someone who needs some help and has called our company. A few years ago someone called from Missouri (we are in Arizona) thinking we were a local company in his area. He had a problem and needed to talk to a technician. We had one of our technicians' call him back and spend over half an hour with him. This man ended up calling him back two other times. Did we make any money on that? No, not a dime on that particular transaction. The payoff is the good will we have created with someone concerned about the safety of his employees and the security of his business. That type of goodwill goes a long way and it was quite satisfying when that gentleman took the time to write a hand-written thank you, acknowledging that we helped him for no charge . We don't believe it is always just about making money. It is about giving back, helping those in our community and beyond. That payoff is never ending. In our industry the important thing is keeping people and their families and employees safe. At Moore Security Solutions, it is about the trust our clients put in us knowing that we are honor bound to not violate that trust. It is not just the right thing to do. It is good business.

Rick has lived in the Tucson community for over 30 years. Just like most people who now call Tucson home, Rick came to Tucson for a weeklong vacation and has been here ever since. He loves the beautiful mountains and the sunshine year around making Tucson a very special place to live and work. And golf!

Rick's work background is in the technology industry. He sold high end home stereo systems for many years; then moved over to high end car audio systems. This is the reason he finds the security industry such a terrific field to be involved in. Change is a constant, and technology is the main driver of that change. He loves being an entrepreneur and businessman and is grateful that he is in an industry that does so many positive things for families and the business community.

You can contact Rick at:

Moore Security Solutions – (520)881-2885

www.mooresecuritysolutions.com

11 IT'S TIME TO GET IN THE HABIT
AUTHOR: PAM STEWART

"We are what we repeatedly do. Excellence then, is not a single act, but a habit."
-- Aristotle

Have you ever taken the time to objectively look at your customer service habits? Yes, I said *habits*! It's what we do over and over again. For starters we need to get in the habit of looking at our habits!

My background is healthcare. As the co-founder of a medical office, I have come to understand first hand, the importance of scrutinizing my own customer service habits. Today we are going to make an appointment in an imaginary medical office. Then we will hypothetically walk into this office and together take a look at some excellent customer service habits. Although our experience will be founded in fiction, my hope for you is that you will experience this medical office in your future!

The phone
We call the medical office. The front office staff answers the phone by identifying the name of the practice, her name and then asks how she may help us. Her tone is calm, unhurried and affirming. We tell her our need. She listens carefully. We are a bit uncomfortable because we have never been to this doctor. She asks us some pointed questions to further understand how that office can best serve us. Her kindness is so real we begin to give her personal

information we were only going to share with the doctor. We are so comfortable we even joke with her. She gently encourages us to move forward with making the appointment. We make the appointment. She reminds us of the location of the office and even offers a few landmarks to help us find it. She assures us that all the labs we need from another office will arrive before the appointment (and she keeps her word.) She ends the call by telling us that the office is looking forward to meeting us and that she knows we will get the help we need.

The office

The office is bright and cheerful with a beautiful bouquet of colorful fresh flowers neatly resting on an antique side table against the wall. The chairs look comfortable. The music makes us think we have entered a relaxing spa. Our eyes are drawn to a little outdoor atrium in the middle of the lobby with a running waterfall and gorgeous blooming plants. A warm, friendly voice welcomes us and directs us to the front desk to sign in. There are 2 smiling women behind the front desk who call us by our names while engaging us in conversation about our doctor visit. They tell us that they were looking forward to meeting us. One of the women identifies herself as the one we spoke to on the phone. We are warmly invited to sign in. One of the staff members actually walks us to the lobby, tells us the doctor is running on time and invites us to take a seat while handing us some reading material. We sit down and relax. While thumbing through one of the magazines, we look up to see one of the staff members holding a fresh cup of water for each of us. She points us to the location of the nearest restroom and the location of the decanter with more fresh water. She again welcomes us and asks if there is anything we might need to be more comfortable. We say that we are fine and thank her. The interesting wall art and beautiful flooring draws our attention to all the details of the office. We catch the eye of another staff member who notices our interest in the ambience of the office. We are invited to take a tour of the office with her because we had extra time before our appointment was scheduled to begin. The tour is phenomenal. We learn all about all the services available at the center and even get to meet 2 other doctors while passing them in the hallways. We are looking forward to our appointment!

Let's examine 7 habits of excellence.

#1 habit of excellence- **Care about your customers, deeply.**
"People will forget what you said, people will forget what you did, but people will never forget how you made them feel." Maya Angelou
"A customer is the most important visitor on our premises. He is not dependent on us. We are dependent on him. He is not an interruption in our work. He is the purpose of it. He is not an outsider in our business. He is part of it. We are not doing him a favor by serving him. He is doing us a favor by giving us an opportunity to do so." – Mahatma Gandhi

Often we walk into a work place and feel like we are an interruption. Have you ever felt that way? My guess is that it is not intentional nor is it directed at us personally. It is simply that the staff has not made a habit of assessing priorities before the day begins. Yes, the copy machine is out of paper. Yes, the phone is ringing off the hook. Yes, there are patients leaving the same time as those arriving. Yes, there are things the staff is anxious to share with each other. Yes, things appear to be falling apart. Regardless of what is going on in the office, the first priority will always be the first priority…. the patient!

Have you ever been treated so rudely on the phone by a staff member that you decided you weren't ever going to step into that office? If you don't care about the person on the phone, they won't care about what you say you can do to help them. The tone of your voice, the rate of speed of your speech, your inflections and your choice of words say 1 of 2 things—I deeply care or I don't care at all…period. Make it a habit to pick up the phone imagining it is your dearest friend who needs your help. You can make a difference and you will!

#2 habit of excellence- **Smile and keep smiling**
"A man without a smiling face must not open shop." Chinese Proverb

It doesn't matter to your patient what is going on in your personal life. They just want affirmation that they have made the right decision walking into your establishment. Your smile will chase away any internal conflict they may have about being in that place, your place. In my home, my husband doesn't smile naturally. He has a smiling heart but it just doesn't always make it to his face. Often people stay back a bit from interacting with him because they are unsure if he really wants to engage in conversation with them. When I brought that to his attention he was surprised because what you were seeing on his face was not reflecting in any way what was going on in his heart or head. He now practices "intentional" smiling and has seen how his unconscious grimace impacted people in ways he had never intended. A smile tells those around you that they are welcome to approach you. It says that you are a safe person to engage in conversation. Taking it one step further, it is important to realize that your smile reflects more than you, it reflects your *entire* business. When a patient walks through the door you want to ensure the experience is phenomenal and that starts with one simple thing.....a smile.

P.S. A smile is as clear over the phone as it is in person.

#3 habit of excellence- **Get to know your customer**
"The more you engage with customers, the clearer things become and the easier it is to determine what you should be doing." John Russell- President of Harley Davidson

A patient is not a paycheck. They are the heartbeat of your business. Learn their names, their kid's names and some fun fact about their lives. I always loved to experience the joy of watching a patient share their photos of that once in lifetime vacation or their newest grandbaby. It moved my heart in deep ways to learn about the death of a loved one so we could get flowers or a card out to the family.
Sometimes getting to know the patient is a simple as learning that fresh flowers cause more allergy problems than no flowers at all or that the music you are playing is depressing to them. In business it really is all about…them!

#4 habit of excellence- **Never stop training your staff**
"Ask yourself 2 questions: What if we train our staff and they leave? What if we don't train our staff and they stay?"Johnism

"Do what you do so well that they will want to see it again and bring their friends." Walt Disney

The first thing to remember when you hire your staff is that all the training in the world won't change a heart that doesn't love people. Questions about loving people were the first questions I would ask when interviewing candidates. The line of questioning would go like this: Do you love people? What does that look like in a workplace? What if the patient doesn't like YOU? The best advice I ever received came from a woman who owned a caretaking facility. She said "Whenever you are around a person in a funk …love them MORE. After all, who can resist that…?" That philosophy is the foundation for platinum customer service and will impact not only your patients but your own work culture in powerfully positive ways. Another piece of advice that spoke volumes to me in my business was "Hire slow and fire fast." If you find that you have hired someone who doesn't love people…let them go. It won't improve over time and in the end they may negatively impact the energy in the office for a long time even after they are gone. It is also true that even a loving staff may not really understand the critical importance of superior customer service. They will need your help. Yes, I said *help*. Outstanding customer service is not something you can successfully *demand. The best way to motivate your staff to better serve is for you to serve your staff better.* Training is an ongoing mindset that starts before the staff ever interfaces with a single patient. It continues outside of a specific training class as they watch you demonstrate it in front of them day after day. It is just as important to point out when your staff is doing something extraordinary for your patients as it is to challenge them to make improvements. Continuously being plugged into the needs of your staff in regards to training allows for you to create teachable moments to instruct them in the moment.

I learned an important customer service lesson one day when I was checking out a very sick patient and her husband. I had her chart opened in front of me while I was entering the supplements she needed for her treatment into our payment system. Out of the blue she began to yell at me for having her chart open as I was not the doctor. In truth, I had the authority to use the chart in that manner but in that moment that was just a detail to be left unsaid. I closed the chart immediately and apologized sincerely. I picked up the closed chart and walked it to her doctor. She watched every move I made. I asked him to open her chart and finish giving me the list of supplements I needed to finish constructing her invoice. He carefully listed them for me and handed the closed chart back to me. My staff commented on that incident for a long time. They were angry at the patient for being so rude to me. It was time for training. I learned an important lesson too. Although a part of me wanted to say that I had every right to look at the Treatment Plan in her chart, I emotionally took a step back. This wasn't about me. It was about the patient. She needed to feel safe and for some reason I had to find a way to provide that to her. I told my staff that when we hold charts, we are virtually holding someone's precious life. Things changed in our office. The charts took on a new special place in our office and in the lives of the staff. That patient asked especially for me to check her out each time she was in the office. The day we stop training and learning is the day we stop achieving excellence in patient care.

#5 habit of excellence- **Love your staff and your work.**
"Always treat your employees exactly as you want them to treat your best customers." Stephen Covey
"Your work is going to fill a large part of your life, and the only way to be truly satisfied is to do what you believe is great work, the only way to do great work is to love what you do." Steve Jobs

I love people so this has always come naturally to me. Your staff is your family. Remember their birthdays. Celebrate special occasions together. Here are some important truisms to remember: Hand out hugs when needed and a stern directive when appropriate. Pay them well and reward them often.   Listen to your staff. Don't gossip and don't let gossip seep into the office because it is a cultural cancer that can't be eradicated easily. Lead with a carrot and not with a stick. Speak well of your staff at all times. Behave with integrity even when no one will know it or even care.

Your work needs to be an outpouring of your passion. There is nothing more exhilarating than being surrounded by the joy that exudes from someone that loves their work. This is not a fake it until you make it situation. When you believe from the depths of your soul that what you are doing will impact someone's life, you become a magnet to those that are seeking your service!

#6 habit of excellence- **Make sure your word matters!**
"Well done is better than well said." Ben Franklin

It is easy to think that once a patient always a patient. That is a lie. The truth is that once a patient the real work begins to *keep* them as a patient. There are a lot of moving parts to excellent patient care and it all starts with being a person of your word. We use to be a culture where a handshake meant something sacred. We stopped shaking hands a long time ago. Now we often casually promise or commit to doing something we are only slightly intending to fulfill. Even if it is time to go home after an unusually busy day, your job is not done until you have done your job. When you say you are going to call a patient as soon as their labs come in --you must be a person of your word. Call them! If you promise to track down transcripts from other doctor's offices -- keep your word. Track them down! It is imperative that you never over-promise and under-deliver. The work day is not over until every promise has been kept. Why would you trust an office that says all the right things but doesn't do any of those things right?

#7 habit of excellence- **Constantly check in.**
"Your customer doesn't care how much you know until they know how much you care." Damon Richards

Every day I made a list of patients that I called to "check in". Some were patients we hadn't seen in awhile while others were patients that I knew were struggling and just needed a kind word in their day. Often times I would be on the phone most of the day learning about what was going on in the lives of our patients. I heard about family financial struggles, impending divorces and possible next treatments for very sick patients. When people were not home I left encouraging voice mails and most of the time I would get a call back. People love to be loved. The phone is just one way to touch lives. Send out cards that say "Thinking about you", "Happy Birthday", "Happy Anniversary" or "Happy Holiday". The way you care for your patients is the way you will grow your business into something extraordinary.

Platinum customer service is all about developing excellent habits. The most meaningful habits to form are those that reflect your genuine love for people. Extraordinary customer service isn't about out doing the next guy. It's about out doing ourselves.

"There is nothing noble in being superior to your fellow man; true nobility is being superior to your former self." Ernest Hemingway

My name is Pam Stewart. I am the co-founder of Salutora. Our business goal is to provide employers with the most up to date, comprehensive and accurate health care resource available to date. Salutora is designed to impact the health of both employers and their employees in significant ways. Employers will experience substantial health care savings. Employees will have access to an empowering, easy to understand, never before available resource that will enable them to make the best possible health care decisions. It's time every business entered the health care information age with confidence. It's time to discover how Salutora will impact your business and your life!

Our website is, www.salutora.com, or feel free to contact me at salutora8@gmail.com or 480-229-4846.

12 THE "A, B, C'S" OF CUSTOMER SERVICE
AUTHOR: GAYA ZEITER

Customer service is the goal of every business but how many businesses actually achieve it? Most business owners know that building a loyal customer base is the secret to a profitable bottom line but achieving that goal can be difficult without a plan to achieve it. If customer service means providing a quality product or service at a fair price; probably most businesses do that or they would not continue to be in business. But if true customer service is exceeding expectations and creating raving fans; that's a much bigger task and very rare to find.

The goal of every business is to drive intense customer loyalty so that those customers would not even consider another source for the product or service. Acquiring new customers is very time consuming, difficult and often expensive. But losing a good quality customer is even more expensive. When they are a raving fan, the option to leave is reduced to very little chance. In this day and age, time is money and searching for a new vendor or source for a product or service is time consuming and unnecessary when highly satisfied with the product/service already being provided.

So how does a business create raving fans? Don't focus on the product or service – focus on the customer experience. Everything that the customer comes into contact with needs to be positive. Here are some ideas to consider.

The first contact a customer has is often via a telephone call or an email request. Are your phones answered by a positive, helpful human voice or an automated system? Do you respond to email or website requests in a timely manner? If there is minimal human contact and delayed responses to requests, the customer is going to assume that their project or order isn't of value to the business and probably take it elsewhere. Just like all of us when we first meet someone, businesses usually only have one chance to make a positive impression. With so many businesses choosing to automate their phones and use voice mail, the business that responds promptly with a human who can answer questions and offer suggestions is a rare commodity. That starts a positive customer experience.

What about the business that has a retail location where the customer can actually purchase onsite? What is the first impression when a customer enters the property and the front door? Is the parking area and landscaping neat and tidy? Are there plenty of handy parking spaces? Is the entrance welcoming and easy to navigate? Is the customer greeted by a friendly and helpful employee? Remember that everything matters when making a first impression. Are work stations organized and clean? Is lighting bright and cheerful? If music is playing, is it soft and pleasant or loud and harsh? Think about every step that a customer might take in doing business with you and eliminate any frustrations. Hiring top-notch employees and taking good care of them makes for a very positive work environment which in turn, makes for good customer service. Grouchy or self-centered employees are usually focused on themselves and rarely provide that extra level of service that builds a loyal customer. Who hasn't been in a fast food drive-through where the order taker offers no greeting, barely understands the order, and shoves the food out the window with no acknowledgement or thank you. How many of us would love to let the business owner know how their customers are being treated but most of us just take our food (hoping the order is at least right!) and move on. We may return again another day but if we have another option, we will most likely try it. We are definitely not a raving fan.

Sometimes problems occur when delivering a product or service, and the way the problem is handled can help secure a positive relationship or can jeopardize it. It is never helpful to get into a confrontation with a customer and take sides. You may win the argument but will probably lose the customer, and unless you want that customer to take his business elsewhere, then you lose too. Focus on the solution to the problem making it clear that you are committed to resolving the problem. Playing the blame game will never result in a positive outcome.

What are some specific things that a business can do to let customers know how appreciated they are? Probably the easiest and most important is to establish a relationship which starts by calling the customer by name. A personal greeting by phone or in person goes a long way in letting the customer know they are remembered and valued. As time goes by, hopefully you will learn some personal details such as family members, favorite activities, previous jobs or education that you can then ask about. Knowing someone has taken the time to get to know you and care about your life makes a very strong connection that is difficult to break. If you can learn customers' birthdays, then mark the date in your calendar and send a card or a small gift to let them know you've remembered their special day. Or take a small holiday like Valentine's Day or St. Patrick's Day and deliver a bag of goodies to celebrate the day. Maybe the first day of spring would be a good time to deliver a tulip or rose especially if it has been a difficult winter season. What a big impression a small effort will make.

Notice that up to this point we have not mentioned the product or service, its price, or its use. These factors are important when a customer is first choosing to buy from you, but they have little relevance to developing an ongoing relationship. Obviously, the customer wants the product or service from someone – the question is why are they choosing you and what will make them choose you over and over again? The answer is all about the relationship. We've all heard that relationships are built on the foundation of "know, like, and trust" and this is very true. We first have to get to know one another, then like one another, then trust one another. But there is one more step that needs to be part of the plan and that is to commit to one another. When we as business owners make the commitment to take care of our customers with no reservation or qualification; those customers will make the same commitment to keep their business with you. And no slick-talking salesman or lower price from another company will change their mind.

Here's an example: Our business is to provide printing and bulk mailing services for small to medium sized businesses. This can range from business stationery to marketing materials; business forms to manuals – anything a business might need to facilitate their operations or promote the marketing of their business. These are products that every business needs in one form or another so every business is a good target for competitor printers to try to move to their company. But when that business has a personal relationship with their printer and considers many of the employees friends and knows that his/her printing project will receive special attention and be delivered early or at the latest, on time; why would they consider trying someone else where these variables would be unknown? One of our business goals at Premier Printing is to "under-promise" and "over-deliver". This means that we always try to surprise the customer with receiving their order early and often with more than they ordered. We proof read customer artwork so simple mistakes can be corrected before printing; we call with suggestions for improvement if we see them. If a photo is less than optimum, we take the time to improve it if we can. Our goal is to deliver a product that we are proud of so we know the customer will be happy too.

Sometimes employees leave a company and a new relationship has to be created. This change can happen either with the customer or with the employees of the business providing the product or service. The first problem is knowing when a personnel change has happened. If it's the customer who normally places the order, it is critical to know as soon as possible when that person may be leaving or when they have left. Often the new contact may have their own ideas about who they want to do business with and since there is no relationship established, it is easy to make a change. When there is an employee change with the providing business, it is easy to make that know to existing customers and start creating relationship opportunities. A good place to start is to visit current customers and do a face-to-face introduction. Spend a few minutes getting to know each other is time well spent. Another option is to invite customers to your place of business for a tour or for a happy hour or lunch get-together. Setting up a teaching event with a popular topic and speaker can also be a good way to bring in good current and potential customers. Doing all of these just provides more opportunities to establish that relationship.

An important step in this process is identifying those customers that you want to become raving fans. Of course we want to provide top level of service to all customers, but realistically, to provide "knock your socks off" service requires all hands on deck and a focus that probably isn't realistic to maintain across the board. So who deserves this extra level of attention? What customer characteristics merit being at the top of the list? An easy way to categorize your customers is to put them on "A", "B", and "C" lists. An "A" customer is top notch, always pays on time (or early), orders regularly and is always a pleasure to work with. A "B" customer pays on time but doesn't order at the volume of the "A" customer. A "C" customer may be a late payer, not a regular customer, and occasionally difficult to work with. All three levels should receive standard good service but obviously any extra customer treatment options should be focused on the "A" customers. But keep in mind that you never know when a "B" or "C" customer will become an "A" customer, and that's when that customer relationship needs the extra attention to move it forward toward higher profitability and longevity.

In creating positive customer relationships, the most critical factor is communication. When communication fails, the foundation of the relationship is likely to fail. Problems are always magnified when one side or the other does not keep the other informed. Sometimes customers change their mind about what they want to order or decide on a different timeline for the delivery. Or on the other end, sometimes problems occur with the production of the order causing a delay or a change in the timing of the delivery. When that information is not communicated between both sides, what might have been a small problem that could be easily handled becomes a major difficulty and often jeopardizes the relationship. There's no excuse for not keeping each other informed in this day and age of email and text messaging. This is where the trust factor comes into play in a good relationship – both sides know that they can trust each other to keep information flowing and avoid any major or minor glitches. Take advantage of the internet to keep in touch – social media is a great way to get connected with your best customers and then use regular updates, likes, and shares to stay connected. It's all about regular touches whether they are face to face, via phone or email, or on the web to keep that communication and interaction flowing.

So we can all agree that customer service is a critical factor in the success and profitability of a business but taking that service to the next level is what makes a business truly successful. Don't take your best customers for granted and assume they will always be there. Many businesses have failed because their customer base was very small (when over 25% of a business' revenue comes from one customer). Ideally no one customer should be more than 5% of the total income of a business so if/when that customer disappears, it is not devastating to business survival. Get started today - identify your top ten customers and then set up a plan to start treating them like gold. Then your business will start reaping the benefits.

Gaya Zeiter has owned Premier Printing and Mailing since 1992. A graduate of Illinois State University with a B.A. degree and Northern Illinois University with a M.Ed degree, Gaya spent 15 years in the education industry prior to owning a business. Premier is a Tucson-owned company serving business customers who want to increase their market share through professional marketing materials, business stationery, forms and direct mail services. Since 1992, Premier Printing & Mailing has offered professional design, printing, full color or black/white copying & automated mailing services with the expertise and technology to print and process bulk mailings so they comply with all postage regulations and receive the lowest postage rates available.

Contact Premier at (520)322-0300 or www.premierprintmail.com.

13 SUMMARY

Now that you have gotten a peek at how some very successful businesses not only strive to, but actually deliver, Platinum Customer Service, all of the co-authors in this book sincerely hope that this inspires you to adopt some of the tricks, techniques and systems into your business and life. In today's business world with the speed at which everything changes such as technology, how we conduct daily business, and how we communicate; it is critical that we reinvent our business practices often in order to be current, timely, and competitive in the marketplace. There is no better way to learn how to reinvent oneself and their business than by studying how other successful businesses have done and are doing it. After you spend any length of time studying the methods of the highly successful, you will find, as you might have discovered in this book, customer service doesn't have to be complicated or even difficult to do well. You just have to make a commitment to study, learn, grow and commit to excellence. As a matter of fact, you will find that if you adopt some of the principals, habits and systems of the ultra-successful, reinventing yourself isn't that difficult at all. The best part is, even if you do adopt some of the principals, habits and systems of others, it's not as though you are stealing their principals, habits and systems; you are just doing what is proven to work and that is honesty, loyalty (to your customer and to your brand) and integrity. Doing the right thing is what makes your customer service, platinum customer service.

On behalf of all the co-authors of this book, we want to wish you all of the success in the world with your businesses, and we want you to trust that you can contact any of us for guidance and leadership because that's just the kind of customer service we are used to providing.

ABOUT THE AUTHORS

This book was conceived as a collaborative effort and was authored by members of the Tucson Marketing Professionals business and marketing organization in Tucson, Arizona. This group has only been in existence for a few years but has gathered the best of the best in entrepreneurs and business owners in their respective fields. At the end of each chapter you will find a short biography of the author as well as information on how to contact them.